FINDING YOUR WAY
after the
SUICIDE *of*
SOMEONE YOU LOVE

FINDING YOUR WAY
after the
SUICIDE *of*
SOMEONE YOU LOVE

DAVID B. BIEBEL, DMin, &
SUZANNE L. FOSTER, MA

ZONDERVAN.com/
AUTHORTRACKER
follow your favorite authors

ZONDERVAN

Finding Your Way after the Suicide of Someone You Love
Copyright © 2005 by David B. Biebel and Suzanne L. Foster

Requests for information should be addressed to:

Zondervan, *Grand Rapids, Michigan* 49530

Library of Congress Cataloging-in-Publication Data

Biebel, David B.
   Finding your way after the suicide of someone you love / David B. Biebel, Suzanne
L. Foster.
      p.   cm.
   Summary: "This resource provides encouraging and practical help and hope for
those left behind after the suicide of a loved one" — Provided by publisher.
   Includes bibliographical references.
   ISBN 978-0-310-25757-8
   1. Suicide. 2. Bereavement — Psychological aspects. 3. Suicide — Religious aspects —
Christianity. 4. Suicide victims — Family relationships.
   I. Foster, Suzanne L. II. Title.
   HV6545.B477   2005
   248.8'66 — dc22   2005002065

Interior design by Beth Shagene

Printed in the United States of America

For Shannon and Jonathan,
whose untimely deaths caused our paths to cross
so we could help others find their way
on a journey none of us would choose.

For all our collaborators,
anonymous and otherwise,
who chose to tap their pain once more
to help their fellow strugglers understand
and more than survive suicide loss.

Acknowledgment: All of the stories in this book are true. Sometimes our collaborators allowed us to use their real names and the names of those they lost to suicide. The following is a list of the names which are real: Mike, Louise Wirick, Monica, Brenda, Becky, Lenore, Debbie, Judy K., Marie, Kathie, Terri, Judy T., James, Patricia, Ginger, Florence, Robert Walters Sr., Linda Flatt, Ann, Mark Wilson, Marlene, Margaret Stephens, Steve Foster, Jerry, Colleen, and Jan. In all other cases, pseudonyms are used to protect the identities and privacy of those who died and those who love them. Any similarity to other persons, living or dead, is coincidental.

We also wish to thank the following for their professional input, and for giving us permission to use their material: Bob Deits, Pleasant Gill White, PhD, Dr. Harold Koenig, Randy Christian, Steve Siler, and Scott Krippayne.

Voice: When we say "we," we are speaking jointly. When we are speaking singly, we will use first names, Sue or Dave, in parentheses to identify the speaker.

Contents

1. Why? Why? Why?   9

2. Wandering and Wondering   21

3. Guilt, the Blight of Broken Hearts   35

4. The Wall   47

5. Depression, the Scourge of Broken Hearts   61

6. Preserving Relationships in the Aftermath of Suicide   79

7. Suicide Survival in Special Situations   91

8. After the Suicide of Your Brother or Sister   105

9. Questions That Remain   117

10. Survival—and Beyond   133

11. Embracing Your New Normal   147

Supplemental Chapter: How to Help Survivors of Suicide   165

Appendix 1 Depression Self-Check   173

Appendix 2 Starting Over: Weaving New Dreams Together   175

Appendix 3 Choosing a Christian Therapist:
            Suggestions and Guidelines   179

Notes   181

Resources and Recommended Reading   187

A Thousand Whys

I look into the Father's eyes
And wrestle with a thousand whys
Why this? Why now? Why him, not I?
The hurt, the rage, unbridled pain
Erupting from my soul, again.
If that's the way it's going to be
Then build Your Kingdom without me.

But then, again, where could I go
To hear a word of hope, and know
The promise that beyond the pain
The ballad has a glad refrain?
But what for now? And how can one
Still vocalize "Thy will be done"?

And soon I hear a song begin,
Celestial, but from deep within,
A new yet ancient melody
Of joy *and* pain, disharmony.
Or do the strains combine somehow,
A lovely paradox of sound?

—DAVID B. BIEBEL[1]

CHAPTER 1

Why? Why? Why?

What do you mean, she's dead?

The words echoed through the chasms of my quickly numbing mind, but I (Sue) couldn't make them come out of my mouth as I struggled to make sense of what the woman on the phone was saying.

How can you know she's dead when you aren't even here?

We had called 911 because we couldn't get nineteen-year-old Shannon to wake up. Steve, her brother, was trying to do CPR. It was all very strange. She had a smile on her face. Her body was warm. But her color was wrong, very wrong.

She's my daughter. She can't be dead. She can't be dead.

"Hello," the voice said. "Are you still there?"

"Yes," I mumbled.

"A team is on the way, ma'am. But let me ask again. Can you find a pulse?"

I looked at Steve. He shook his head, with tears in his eyes. "No. We can't."

"Then the girl is dead," the voice said again. "There's nothing you can do."

How can you pronounce her dead as calmly and callously as you might announce the time or the weather? I wondered. My voice said, "Thank you," my hand hung up the phone, and part of me disconnected from the rest of myself.

By the time the medical personnel arrived, I felt like I was hovering somewhere near the ceiling, a spectator at some kind of macabre dramatic performance in which my intuition said I had a lead part, only I didn't know the script. *What are all these people doing here?* I wondered. *Why does the phone keep ringing? Why is everyone so sad . . . especially Steve?*

And Shannon, my dear, beautiful Shannon.

I watched as they wrapped her up and whisked her away, without even giving me a chance to say goodbye. Didn't they know that I needed to touch her, to look at her, to remember her, to say goodbye?

And my mind cried out: *Who could have done such a horrible thing to her — five days before Christmas? Why, we haven't finished decorating the tree. And the shopping isn't done. I haven't bought Shannon her special ornament yet. This is just a bad dream, and I'm going to wake up soon.*

"Ma'am, excuse me," a policeman's voice interrupted my nightmare. "We found these by her bed."

He showed me all the empty bottles — Shannon had taken all the prescription medication in the house, plus a half bottle of aspirin — and that was when it finally dawned on me that Shannon had done this horrible thing . . . to herself.

Many Questions, Few Answers

But why? What could have been so painful for her that death seemed better than life?

My last words to Shannon the night before had been harsh and unkind. She had come in late from a date with her boyfriend and was making a lot of noise, which woke me up. "Can you please keep the noise down?" I had yelled. "I'm trying to sleep."

And her last words to me were, "It's okay, Mom. It will be all right now."

Of course, I hadn't known what she was thinking. But for months afterward, I imagined myself responsible, somehow, for her death.

Steve and I both wondered for a long time, since we were both in the house when she took the pills, *Why didn't we hear her? Why didn't we know? Why didn't God alert us in some way to what was about to happen?*

The last question was perhaps harder than the others, even though none of the questions had answers. After all, we were believers — all three of us. Surely a good God wouldn't allow such a thing to happen. How could he? Children don't die before their parents; it's not right. Didn't he know that Shannon was to graduate from college, get married, give me grandchildren, and bury *me* at a ripe old age? This was senseless. *You knew, God, before time began that this*

was going to happen. Why her? Why us? Why me? Why did you give me this child,
only to take her away?

All day and into the night, people came in and went. My boss drove all the way from Palm Springs straight to my house (near San Diego) when he heard the news. He had loved Shannon like a daughter and was devastated. I felt loved and cared for by so many people who came and tried to make sense out of something so senseless. I was numb, in shock, and just let people take care of me. I needed to talk and appreciated those who just listened. I ignored the ones who didn't know what to say or who tried to comfort me with comments like, "She's with the Lord; it must have been God's will," "Thank God you still have Steve because he will really need you now," and, "God works all things together for good."

I wanted to scream back, "This is not God's will, and there is nothing good about this." The words lay formless in my mouth.

At one point my pastor said, as gently as he could, that we needed to think about funeral arrangements. *Oh no. No funeral arrangements, because if I make funeral arrangements, it must mean she is really dead, and, God, if I go to sleep and wake up, you will make everything all right, won't you? I mean, if I'm really good, you will make this story end the way I want it to, right?*

I wanted to die. I couldn't imagine feeling any more pain than I was already feeling. "All of you leave and just let me go to sleep and not wake up" was what I wanted to say. Others must have known this, because I was not left alone. Someone was with me around the clock for the next four days, taking care of my every need—except for my most desperate need: to have my broken world put back together again.

And the biggest heartbreak of all was to see the agony on my son's face and not be able to fix it. I was a mother, a lousy, horrible mother, with one child who had taken her own life and another in so much pain that I feared he might follow his sister, and there was *nothing* I could do about any of it. *What kind of mother would let these things happen to her children?*

I hoped that if I could just go to sleep that night, the demons would leave me alone, and just maybe, a merciful God would put everything back together the way it was. I was wrong. There was no peace with sleep. The demons haunted my dreams.

Implosion

I awoke the next morning feeling like I had been hit with a wrecking ball, convinced that I could not survive this. Someone had said the day before that time would heal this. Time? Didn't they know that *nothing* could heal this? I couldn't imagine surviving the next second, much less the next hour or the next day.

My pastor called to say that my ex-husband had started making arrangements for the funeral and that I needed to go to the funeral home to go over the details. *How was he, the father of my children, able to do this?* I wondered. *What special ability enabled him to do this again in the wake of the loss of his stepdaughter only months before?*

So I gathered up Shannon's favorite ring, her favorite outfit, and a few items that would be placed in her casket with her. I was so grateful that I didn't have to make any other decisions and that others had made the important ones for me.

The funeral would be on Monday afternoon, December 23, for family and a few close friends. My task was to plan a memorial service for that evening, which would be open to all those who knew her and us. Oh, this was something I could do all right, because I'm a planner. I just knew that if I kicked into high gear I could cover the agony I was feeling by planning a memorial service that would be remembered by all.

On Sunday morning, a dear friend took me out for breakfast at a lovely seaside restaurant in La Jolla. There was no way I could attend church and hear the announcement of her death. I couldn't cope with that or deal with the people afterward. I don't remember anything about that breakfast except that I couldn't bear to eat the food that was placed in front of me. For two days, I had walked and talked in a zombie-like trance, and day three was no different.

Monday threatened rain—weather to match the storm raging in my heart. My parents arrived, and once again, I went over all the details. *Would the telling never end?* We talked about Shannon, remembering things about her life, some long forgotten. Strangely, I found talking about her and hearing others share their memories of her very comforting. It kept her alive, if only in our hearts.

Before the funeral, I spent a couple of hours with my pastor and his wife, planning the memorial service. Some of Shannon's friends from church that she had grown up with planned to sing Michael W. Smith's song "Friends," from the musical they had performed when they were all in high school. Shannon had had a lead part in the musical. I planned to talk about Shannon and asked some of her closest friends to do that also. Others planned to share their memories during an open time of sharing. I had selected music that I knew she and others liked. Various families in the church were providing food for out-of-town guests. It was a well-thought-out service, but one I really didn't want to attend.

More than three hundred people attended the memorial service that evening. Some had traveled great distances to be there. I so appreciated their thoughtfulness. I remember thinking: *How did they all know about this? How did they find out?*

I survived the funeral and the memorial service as if in a trance. Except for the grace of God and the support of some very dear friends, I could not have endured it.

My family stayed to be with Steve and me through Christmas. We somehow managed to open the gifts under the tree, though each gift from Shannon brought more tears.

Friends came by, bringing what comfort and help they could. But nothing eased the horrible ache in my heart for a long, long time.

Survivors

A survivor of suicide is anyone who has been affected by the loss of someone to suicide—parent, spouse, child, sibling, or friend. "It's an exclusive club I joined without wanting to," one survivor told us. "But I passed the initiation, so I guess I'm a member."

Following a loved one's suicide, many questions haunt the survivors, the most common of which start with why, such as: Why did my loved one choose death over life? Why didn't I see it coming? Similar questions are common to other losses, as expressed by Dave's poem "A Thousand Whys," written after his three-year-old son died from an undiagnosed illness. When a loved one's death was self-inflicted, however, some of the questions that linger the longest relate to the one who has died.

I (Sue) asked the why question over and over in the days, weeks, and months following Shannon's death: Why would a beautiful, intelligent, well-liked young woman take her own life? Those of us who were closest to her discussed this endlessly, trying to come up with answers. While there didn't appear to be one specific predisposing factor, except that she had been severely depressed, which led to hopelessness and despair, just talking about it helped each of us to deal with her death, and ultimately to heal. As her brother, Steve, told me after her death, she had lost all hope and her will to live.

While some survivors can answer the why questions with some certainty, many cannot. For who really knows what goes on in the minds of those who end their pain in this way? For some of them, it may be family issues, financial problems, difficulties in school or work, relationship issues, gender-identity issues, addictive behaviors, or physical disabilities, all of which may be intensified by depression and/or other mental or emotional disorders. As many survivors have told us, they needed to talk through the why questions with trusted others in the early stages after the loss.

Many survivors eventually come to a point in their healing when the why questions become less important and "Where do we go from here?" becomes the focus. Linda Flatt, who lost her twenty-five-year-old son to suicide, wrote, "The only person (except for God) with the answers to my questions is unavailable to hear them. And it occurs to me that he might not know the answers himself." She added that after so many years, perhaps it was time to stop asking the questions, realizing that she really didn't want answers as much as she wanted a chance to challenge the answers and to change the outcome.[2]

Over time, the questions change from inquiries that begin with "why" to questions that begin with "what," "who," and "how." Ultimately your questions may begin to focus on how your experience may be able to help others: "What do you want me to do with what I've learned, God?" or "Who needs a word of hope today?" or "How can I best walk alongside that hurting person I met the other day?" This change takes awhile. It may take a long while. Though you may feel your progress is slow, it's best to remember that healing from a loss like yours is an inside-out process, overseen by the ultimate heart-mender, God.

What to Expect during the First Few Days

Note: If you've already survived this period, we trust it will encourage you to know that your emotions and reactions were normal.

You will experience shock. Emotional numbness is a normal reaction to trauma, the mind and body's way of protecting you from the full force of the trauma. People in shock feel like they are in a fog, disconnected from themselves and the world around them—as if they're in a trance or having a bad dream.

People in shock should delay making decisions that will have lifelong consequences, such as liquidating or giving away assets, as these matters will look different in time.

You will experience severe emotional and/or physical reactions. You may experience anxiety, anger, confusion, flashbacks, fear, chest pains, breathing problems, sleep disturbances, and other disturbances in your normal day-to-day functioning. Such reactions are common after a loved one's suicide but may be intensified depending on the circumstances surrounding the death, such as witnessing the suicide or finding the body.

Tell a close friend or counselor about your symptoms. Seek qualified medical assistance, as there are good medications that can help you without causing long-term dependence.

You will have to deal with the police, medical professionals, the coroner, and others who must be involved after a suicide. Some of these professionals have had training in dealing with suicide and its survivors; many have not. Some may seem insensitive and less than helpful, but it is good to remember that their first responsibility is to deal with the suicide on a factual basis. The police will sometimes be accompanied by a crisis counselor, whose job is to help you deal with the immediate trauma and to give you resources that will help you as you grieve.

Involve your lawyer, pastor, counselor, and other supporters in this process as much as possible since your ability to recall some details may be impaired, and others may be able to help you remember what's been discussed already and what hasn't.

The media may become involved, depending on the circumstances surrounding the death. This seems intrusive, and it may create internal conflict or conflict with others whose opinions about how to handle the media may differ from yours.

Remember that you have no obligation to speak to any member of the media. Some survivors have told us, however, that they were glad they consented to an interview or wrote something for publication, usually done in the hope of preventing other suicides.

You will have to make funeral arrangements if the one who died is a spouse, child, parent, or other person for whom you were responsible.

Ask a friend, pastor, counselor, or someone else whom you trust to help you make decisions about funeral arrangements. One issue you will have to decide is whether you want an open casket, closed casket, or no casket present at all—for example, when cremation or burial has already occurred and the focus of the service is solely to memorialize the one who has died. Research shows that of the survivors who held typical funerals, most of those who chose an open casket felt that this approach brought a sense of reality to what had happened and allowed loved ones to say a final goodbye. In cases of gunshot wounds or other disfiguring methods of suicide, however, a closed casket certainly makes sense.

When making funeral arrangements, the advice of trusted friends can help you avoid choosing options (caskets and other details related to the funeral) that you can't really afford. While your feeling of responsibility for what happened might skew your judgment, consulting with others will bolster your confidence, looking back, that you made the best decisions you could make at the time.

You will have to decide what to tell people about how your loved one died. Survivors who chose to be open about the circumstances surrounding their loved one's death were glad (in retrospect) that they were. Their openness allowed others to minister to them in helpful and appropriate ways. It also helped the survivors in their grieving and healing process to be able to speak truthfully about what happened.

You will find that some people will allow you to talk openly about the suicide of your loved one and will respond in a supportive way, which increases your ability to comfortably share the circumstances surrounding the death.

Others, however, even close friends, will not be able to deal with any aspect of the situation and won't want to let you talk about it, thus piling pain on top of pain. You have to learn who is safe and who isn't, who you can talk to and who won't listen. In any event, talking about it is an important part of healing, and we strongly recommend finding someone who will let you honestly express what you are feeling.

The truth about your loved one's suicide will most likely become known. All the energy and anxiety that a cover-up would require would be better invested in pursuing your own healing.

It may be difficult to accept others' help, perhaps because you want to be "strong," you desire privacy, or you're already depleted and don't want to feel obligated to repay the kindness of others later.

Let others do those "have to" things, such as preparing meals, running errands, or canceling appointments. Let others take care of you in nurturing and comforting ways. It's okay to talk about the loss and to cry until you don't think you can cry anymore. Good friends who love you will understand, and they will not expect their kindness to be repaid.

You will be strongly tempted to try to escape the pain or to dull it in some way. It might start with something as innocuous as a glass of wine to calm your nerves or help you relax. But soon you'll need more and more wine, or even harder stuff, to achieve the same result. This is how addiction begins.

You may even wish you could die to end the pain or to go and be with the one who has died.

If you find yourself longing to escape, tell someone. Start with your physician and/or your counselor, both of whom will understand that these longings are common and are likely symptoms of depression, for which excellent treatments are available. If you had a broken leg, you wouldn't feel guilty accepting medical care. Since you have a broken heart, you need not feel guilty seeking medical, psychological, and spiritual help. By asking for help, you are acknowledging your pain and taking the first steps toward healing.

Today's the Day . . .

Today's the day . . . three months ago
You made the decision to go away,
To end your life and the struggles and pain
Leaving us in a world that will never be the same.

My heart is breaking and the tears flow free
As I try to accept your pain I did not see.
My arms yearn to hold you once again
And to heal the pain and to help you mend.

You made the choice to end it all
And selected the time of a full moon in fall.
We knew you were gone but did not know where;
No clues that we needed to guard our hearts and prepare.

The news that you took your own life away
Will never be forgotten in the blur of that day.
I wonder what your thoughts were as you planned
And made the final preparations with your own hands.

The Lord was there waiting with outstretched hands
To take you and love you in his heavenly lands.
There are times when I feel you close in my space
Your angels' wings gently brushing my face.

And the small signs that you send from above
Provide moments of peace and joy in your love,
To know that one day I'll hold you again in my arms
And we'll both be in a place of no hurt and no harm.

My sorrow and loss will never go away;
My new life will form as I live through each day.
In the Lord's plan I must put all my trust
With thoughts of you watching over us.

I can't imagine life without you here,
The memories I have are now so dear.
My love for you will continue to grow
My words stop here as the tears start to flow.

—ANN, WAYNE'S MOM[1]

CHAPTER 2

Wandering and Wondering

Grief is a natural and normal reaction to the loss of your loved one. Regardless of the expectations of others, or even your expectations of yourself, significant loss brings grief, and the more devastating the loss, the greater the grief and the longer it will likely last.

Your grieving is a process that can't be hurried or ignored. You can't "just get over it," no matter how much you try or how much others want you to. You must go through it to get beyond it. Grieving is hard work, especially when it comes from such a traumatic loss as the suicide of someone you love.

During the first few months after your loved one's death, you will wander through an emotional wasteland as you grieve, experiencing any or all of these components:

Shock and numbness—feeling like you are in a daze or a fog, confusion, disorientation, disbelief and denial of the death, forgetfulness, feeling distracted, difficulty in remembering things, difficulty in focusing on normal tasks, and difficulty in making decisions.

Anger—toward the deceased, self, others, and God.

Fear—of losing another family member to suicide, of becoming suicidal yourself, of going crazy, of ever loving or trusting anyone again, of what others might think or say, and of forgetting your loved one.

Depression—feeling hopeless, feeling that life has no meaning or purpose, not wanting to go on with life, loss of pleasure in normal activities, isolation, continual crying, intense and overwhelming sadness, anxiety, nightmares, feelings of helplessness and being out of control, and

GRIEVING THE LOSS OF A LOVED ONE TO SUICIDE

Ten Myths

1. You will get over it in a month or two.
2. You will handle it like everyone else.
3. You will grieve in the same way as your spouse, your children, or others close to the deceased.
4. You won't be angry at the deceased.
5. You shouldn't cry.
6. You shouldn't talk about the loss.
7. Your marriage, inevitably, will fail.
8. You won't have suicidal thoughts.
9. Your life will never have meaning again.
10. The experience will be a straight-line process through the stages of grief and beyond acceptance to joy again, and the pain will never return.

various new physical symptoms, including: loss of appetite, sleep problems, extreme fatigue, loss of sexual interest, nausea, dizziness, shortness of breath, chest pains, and restlessness.

Guilt—feeling responsible for the death or that you could have done something to stop it, replaying the event over and over and thinking, "if only," or "I should have," or "I could have." You may even feel guilty about being relieved that the problems are finally over and you won't have to deal with them again.

Rejection—abandonment, isolation, loneliness, and feeling that your loved one did this intentionally to hurt you.

Changeability—one day you may think you're recovering; the next you may wish you'd never been born.

As you wander, you will wonder:

- What to tell others about your loved one's death.
- How to handle the reactions of others, especially those who are judgmental.
- Why this happened.
- What to do with your loved one's possessions.
- If you'll ever sort out the crisis-of-faith issues you may be experiencing.
- How to help your family deal with their grief issues.
- Why your family isn't meeting all of your needs.
- How to handle the ups and downs of grieving, the flashbacks, and the constant reminders of the deceased that immerse you in the pain again.

The Spiral Staircase

Stage 3: Mind and Will
- Reality sets in
- Numbness wears off
- Acceptance
- Moving on

Stage 2: Emotions versus Mind
- Confusion
- Conflict
- Vacillation
- Searching for answers
- Intense sadness and pain

Stage 1: Emotions
- Numbness
- Shock
- Disbelief
- Disconnection
- Going through the motions

While it helps to know that you will wonder as you wander through the wilderness called grief, you also need to know that your journey will likely be more circular than linear, and you will revisit certain "places" along the way several times, as if you were climbing a spiral staircase (see illustration).

At the bottom and at the top of the staircase, you're facing in the same direction—which for a believer is toward God. Quite often during the ascent, however, you are facing in a different direction. You may think you've passed a place before (some climbers even chastise themselves over this), but the truth is that each step along your path of grief changes your point of view. For example, let's suppose that on one of the lower steps, you were looking at your anger over what has happened. As you continue to climb the stairs, sooner or later you'll find yourself looking at your anger again, but from a different vantage point. This is not failure (as in, "I thought I had dealt with that already"), but one little-known aspect of the journey of grief.

The First Stage of Grief

The staircase has three sections. The first section includes shock, disbelief, and emotional numbness. During this stage, the mind functions because it must; you make decisions and plans and handle details, sometimes without any feeling whatsoever or even any memory of it later. You may say and do all the "right" things while in this dazed condition, and observers may note that you seem to be "handling it well," when all you are really doing is surviving. In fact, this initial response to trauma seems to be the psyche's way of protecting us from actually feeling the pain to the fullest degree.

Linda described this stage as "being in a thick fog." Ginger said that after the death of her son, Todd, "It was as if someone had taken a sheet of waxed paper and draped it over my face, obstructing my vision."

The Second Stage of Grief

The second section of the spiral staircase is an extended period of internal struggle, sometimes bordering on chaos, in which the emotions battle with the mind for control of the direction in which you wish to go. Although the timing varies according to the individual, this phase generally begins as the emotional numbness wears off, and intense sadness and pain become constant companions.

During this time, it may seem that a wrestling match is going on in your inner self, as the struggle to comprehend what has taken place intensifies. You may feel things you've never felt—rejection, abandonment, betrayal, overwhelming guilt or remorse, sadness beyond imagination, intense anxiety or fear, emptiness like a black hole threatening to suck you in, and anger (even rage) toward the deceased, others, God, even yourself. You may become demanding, irritable, and impatient—with yourself and with others.

You may think things you've never thought—from doubting the goodness of God, to doubting the reality of your faith, to pondering joining that loved one in death. You may conclude that you have lost (or are about to lose) your mind. Back and forth goes the battle within, or in our analogy, round and round the staircase you go, struggling upward toward healing, circling back to revisit the pain.

Your body also will likely reflect your psychic, spiritual, and relational pain. You may experience some or all of these symptoms:

- Hyperactivity or underactivity; restlessness or lethargy
- Chest pains, stomach and abdominal pains, headaches, and other pains
- Shortness of breath
- Changes in appetite, resulting in weight loss or weight gain
- Sleep problems
- Difficulty concentrating
- Memory problems
- Feeling confused or disoriented

Don't ignore your symptoms. They can be signs of depression or of some physical ailment. Seek medical assistance. Tell your doctor what has happened and how your life has changed since the tragedy.

The Third Stage of Grief

The third and top section of the spiral staircase involves your will. As a result of the suicide of your loved one, a certain new reality has become yours; specifically, that this person is no longer part of your ongoing experience of life. Hate it though you may, your mind eventually accepts this new reality to be true. Your emotions, once raw and out of control, have shown you the depth of your love for the deceased. Difficult as your grieving has been, there is now a positive side to this new reality. Your will to live begins to guide your actions. You begin to feel empowered to use what you have learned to help someone else.

While no analogy can perfectly describe grief, we like the image of the spiral staircase because it depicts a factor of grieving that is not expected by most people and is not discussed very often in the literature: grief is somewhat circular (as opposed to a straight-line process, stage to stage until it's over). In reality, for many survivors, the "staircase" becomes a lifelong experience, in which even the joy of helping others may be tempered by the power of certain situations to thrust the survivor into the throes of grief again. Yet even when this happens, the pain is not as severe as before, and the process of recovery is not as long.

I (Sue) had studied the stages of grief, but I was still surprised to find that grief is not linear. After Shannon's funeral and that first Christmas without her, Steve returned to his father's, and so I was left alone to figure out what to do next. I remember taking down the Christmas tree and thinking that I had to make a proactive effort to deal with this loss. It was at that point that I called Focus on the Family to ask for some reading material and a recommendation for a therapist in my area. They gave me both. I just knew that if I could figure this out and understand it, I could get a handle on the process and basically sail through it. Never having lost anyone close to me before, however, all my preparations left me totally unprepared for the emotional roller coaster that was to follow.

Sometimes the pain was so bad I didn't know how I would survive. It was all I could think about when I was awake, and it filled my dreams when I was asleep. I cried. Anything could set me off.

I had been given a card for the Survivors of Suicide organization in San Diego by the crisis team that came to the house on the day of Shannon's death. I attended my first meeting in January. There were people there who had lost loved ones to suicide as far back as *eleven* years. I left. I simply could not sit through that meeting. I knew that if I would still be talking about Shannon's death eleven years later and would still be feeling like I did at that moment, I simply didn't want to live. I didn't go to another meeting for a long time.

During those first few months, I read everything I could about suicide and loss. I learned that what I was going through was normal. This helped me intellectually, but it didn't prepare me for the turmoil in my heart. I also began therapy with a Christian therapist, and while he was not trained or experienced in dealing with a survivor of suicide, having someone to talk to each week was vital for me.

Gradually I was able to make it to a place where my mind could actually focus on something else for a few minutes, but Shannon's suicide was always just underneath the surface, ready to grab me by the throat—again. I lived as if in a haze, watching the world go on around me, mechanically doing what had to be done.

The constant reminders of Shannon kept the pain alive and fresh. So I began cleaning out her room. I didn't want to see all the reminders of her. It was so difficult going through her things, packing things I wanted to keep, giving away those I didn't. While packing her things in the garage, I found a box of clothes I had saved from when she was small. When I pulled out her first soccer shirt with her name on it, I was immediately beamed into a black abyss. I cried for days. But cleaning out her room did help make her death more of a reality.

Shannon's college roommates came to see me. They each took something of hers to remember her by. We shared some wonderful memories of Shannon, but I felt dead and empty after they left, realizing that there would be no more good times with my daughter.

My world had stopped. It was as though I had stepped off, taken a look around, and not liking what I saw, didn't want to get back on. I wanted to scream at relatives and friends as they went on about their business and their lives appeared so normal: "How can you just go on with life? Don't you understand that I don't do normal anymore?"

I bargained with God, hoping this would change things. Then I railed at him when nothing changed. Once I told a friend, "If God doesn't understand my pain, he should consider retiring and letting someone else do his job!"

I also became angry with Shannon. "This was a senseless act of pure rejection of everyone who has ever loved you," I told her. "Why did you do this to me?"

It took me a long time to realize that suicide was something she did to *herself*.

Hindrances to Healing

Others

Forgiving the stupid things that onlookers do or say following a suicide is not as easy as you might imagine. I (Sue) was angry at the insensitivity of others. Not knowing what to say, they often spoke words that they thought were comforting, such as:

"God must have wanted her with him."

"She's in a better place."

"Be happy for the nineteen years you had with her."

Though such comments made me livid, I rarely responded. One, I didn't have the energy for a fight. And two, I was afraid if I got into a fight, I might hurt someone. I didn't need pious platitudes. I needed someone to hold me, share my pain, weep with me, and walk with me through the wasteland into which I'd been transported without a map or even a path to follow. I instinctively knew that I would have to find my own way home, but I had no idea how long it would take.

There comes a time when friends and others who see us regularly just want us to stop grieving. Mike said his boss told him he should get over the death of his son and get on with his life. Louise struggled with similar advice. "The stigma of the word *suicide*," she said, "creates barriers in finding the help survivors need for support and understanding. It is very common for people to react to the word *suicide* in ways that insinuate the survivor must be dirty, contagious, or from an undesirable family. Because of this reaction, some survivors never talk about it or seek the help they desperately need."

Ginger wrote that she was hurt by those who seemed to be tired of her grief and eventually turned their backs on her and walked away. Another survivor said, "Some of our friends stopped speaking to us. At the grocery store in our neighborhood, where we have been shopping for many years, old friends would see us and almost run the other way."

It is not uncommon to find these same attitudes in the church. While some church communities can be very caring, providing the loving support suicide survivors need, others almost shun the survivors. One survivor wrote, "Our church walked away from us. Our pastor wrote us a horrible letter, saying the church wasn't there to minister to us, but we were to minister to them. We left there and didn't return to church for three years." Another survivor said, "The hurtful cruelty of the small group in our church has hindered my healing the most."

I (Sue) received a letter, unsigned but claiming to be from someone in my church, telling me what a horrible mother I'd been and that it was no wonder my daughter did what she did, that I was the cause of her death.

You should expect to hear—and learn to ignore—pious platitudes such as:

"God must love you very much to let you go through this."
"Remember, everything is God's will."
"Your [child, spouse, friend] is better off. She is in heaven and will have eternal peace."
"If you look around, you'll always find someone worse off than you are."
"But you have other children."
"You can always get married again."
"Time heals all heartaches."

People who say such things do not know how to help you. They may be well-meaning enough, but they simply don't comprehend the depth of your pain. For you to heal, it is important to anticipate comments like these and to forgive those who make them—ahead of time.

Ourselves

Not all hindrances come from outside of ourselves. As survivors, we often set up roadblocks or hindrances to our own healing. Some of these include the following.

Not being willing to share our pain. Monica told us that one of the biggest hindrances to her healing has been her unwillingness to share her pain with others. A compassionate and caring counselor, pastor, or other professional can be very helpful if you find this is a problem for you. A caring community of others who have lost a loved one to suicide can also help your healing. It is unusual for a survivor to recover without the support of others.

Unresolved grief. Unresolved grief from past losses may make the current loss more difficult to deal with. I (Sue) was deeply depressed before Shannon died, which complicated and prolonged my grief after she died. It is important to allow yourself to grieve losses as they come. Only by feeling the pain of each loss can you hope to heal from it.

Feeling disloyal if we start feeling better. Another hindrance to our healing is that at some level, although we long for healing of our mind and emotions, we may harbor the notion that letting go of the pain and really living again would somehow be unfaithful to the memory of our loved one who has died. One way to get beyond this is to imagine what that person might say to you. It might go something like this: "Be happy. It's okay. You've been sad enough long enough."

Not being ready to be healed. In the gospel of John, chapter five, there's a story that relates to chronic illness. A man who had been paralyzed for thirty-eight years was lying by the pool called Bethesda, where people came to be healed. It was thought that when an angel stirred the waters, the first one in would be healed. When Jesus saw this man, he asked him, "Do you want to get well?" (v. 6). The man replied that others always beat him into the water because he had no one to help him. Jesus told the man, "Get up! Pick up your mat and walk" (v. 8). And the man was immediately cured.

It is Jesus' question that cuts to the heart of the matter for us as survivors: "Do we want to get well?" Many who endure chronic heartache eventually come to this question: *Am I ready to be whole?* You are the only person who can answer that question for yourself. Though it is unlikely you will ask yourself this question during the first few months, it is possible. And if you hear the voice of Jesus asking you, "Do you want to get well?" humbly say yes to his healing graces.

How Healing Starts

I (Sue) was at my lowest point about four months after Shannon died. The numbness had worn off, and reality had set in. I knew that God promised he would never give us any more than we could handle, but I thought maybe he and I should discuss the disparity between his definition of my limit and my definition. I just didn't think I could go on. In reality, I didn't want to.

The only good thing about the pain I felt after the numbness wore off was that I realized why—if she had felt the pain, hopelessness, and despair that dogged me day by day—she had opted out. I longed to end that pain and went as far as asking to purchase a burial plot next to hers.

At that point God intervened in some truly miraculous ways. While on a trip to Arizona to visit friends, I was given a book on grief written by their former pastor. In the first few pages, I found that he was describing all I had been feeling and going through. I called him and talked to him for quite a while and was so relieved to hear that what I had been experiencing was normal after a suicide. He was surprised that I was doing as well as I was.

When I returned from Arizona, I started a grief recovery class at a local church. This was instrumental in my healing. I continued therapy and found out that I was clinically depressed and probably had been for a long time. I came to see that Shannon also had been depressed. Up to that point, I had not been very well informed about depression. After my own diagnosis, however, I made it a point to find out all I could about this condition—its symptoms, causes, and treatments. In the process, I discovered depression's potentially deadly effect when left untreated (there is a 15 percent suicide rate among those with clinical depression).

Gradually my pain became easier to bear. The peaks and valleys of the grief process began to level out somewhat, and I was able to go longer periods of time between the very deepest lows. It became easier to function at my job. I began to enjoy going out again and spending time with friends. But always in the back of my mind was this question: *Will this wandering and wondering ever stop?*

Things That Will Help You Heal

When we asked a group of survivors to identify what was most helpful to them as they tried to find their way, we received a long list. Some of their answers might be helpful to you.

- "Sharing the experience with other survivors," Brenda wrote. "Reaching out to others who are new to the journey and helping them out of the dark pit at the beginning of the journey."
- "Prayer and worship music brought peace when I felt most desperate," Louise said. "Another thing that helped was to close my eyes and picture myself crawling up on the lap of the Lord, and I would sob those gut-wrenching sobs while the Lord held me."
- "The Survivors of Suicide [SOS] support group has helped the most," Mike said.
- "Talking with people who have been there is so helpful. Helping others as an SOS volunteer is an important part of the process."
- "God's provision and guidance, my own determination to survive, support of family and friends, the ability to pass the hope of my recovery on to other survivors, and the knowledge that I've been able to use my experience to make a contribution in the lives of others" were all helpful to Linda.
- "Educating myself by reading books on suicide, trauma, and recovery," Judy K. said.
- "My love for the Lord and his love for me" sustained Marie.
- "Journaling my thoughts and feelings is one of the things that has helped me the most," Kathie said. "Also, speaking about my loss at schools really helped my healing."
- "Faith. Knowing that even if I felt the grief would overcome me, God still loved me," Terri said. "Also, friendships within the Christian community, hearing others witness about how God's grace helped them through all kinds of adversity and pain reminded me how vast is his love for us."

The First Three to Four Months

· Don't try to make it on your own; accept help and seek it out.
· Talk about your loss and your loved one with supportive, caring people.
· Feel your grief; don't avoid or postpone it.
· Accept the reality of what has happened.
· Give yourself time to grieve; don't rush yourself, and don't let others hurry you.
· Put off making major decisions until you can think clearly, without your emotions interfering with sound judgment.
· Promote your own healing through reading, journaling, and educating yourself about suicide and grieving.
· Take care of yourself physically by getting enough rest, eating the right foods, exercising, and relaxing when you can.
· Be cautious about taking medications or other substances that dull the pain.
· Call on your personal faith and use prayer to help you through this time.
· Visit the cemetery as often as you need to or want to.
· Avoid people who are critical; allow others to help you, including your pets.
· Find a suicide support group, a grief group, a caring and helpful counselor or pastor, or a physician who understands.
· Return to work and normal activities when you are ready to do so, without becoming a workaholic to avoid feeling the pain.
· Reach out and help others when you are ready and able.
· Laugh when you can, for as Proverbs 17:22 says: "A merry heart doeth good like a medicine: but a broken spirit drieth the bones" (KJV).
· Never let go of your hope.

If Only

If only we could have just one more chance;
If only we hadn't lost this one.
What if we could go back in time?
If only we could have saved him.

If only we had fully known his pain;
If only we could begin again.
What if we had a little more time?
If only we had known before.

If only we could have read his mind;
If only we could have eased his pain.
What if he could begin again?
If only we could change the past.

If only we could hug him close,
If only just one more time.
What if we could truly live again?
If only for just a little while.

If only we could forgive ourselves;
If only we could make amends.
What if we were given that chance?
If only we could do it again.

—GINGER BETHKE[1]

CHAPTER 3

Guilt, the Blight
of Broken Hearts

"I should have seen this coming," said Kathie, who lost her son to suicide. "I had a strong bond with Stevie. Shouldn't I have known something like this would happen? If only I had said 'I love you' more often. If only we hadn't made him move out of the house. If only we never had a gun. What if the pastor had kept the appointment with him? I think a person can beat himself to death with these questions."

Mike, who lost a son, wrote: "If only I had not gone out of town that week; if only I could have been a better father; if only I had locked up my truck keys; if only we had never left our home state of Minnesota; if only ... and the list goes on and on and never stops. All the things I, and we as parents, could have or should have done will be with us forever. At this point in our journey, I don't think about them every day as I used to. At first, we spent all our waking moments in the early stages of grief asking these questions of ourselves over and over."

"Paul threatened suicide about six months before he died," Linda recalls. "I addressed the threat but operated under the misconception that if people talk about suicide, they won't do it. When he told me that he was kidding and would never do anything like that, I believed him—I wanted to believe him—and did not pursue the issue. Knowing what I know now, I would have made more of an effort to help, or to get him help. I consider this a realistic mighta. But I also hit myself over the head with many unrealistic shouldas, couldas, and wouldas right after the suicide, mostly having to do with parenting mistakes that I either made or perceived that I made. I shoulda been a better mom. If I coulda been a better mom, my son would be alive. If I woulda been a better mom, my son would not have made the decision to give up on life—and on me."

I (Sue) felt I should have known that something was wrong, should have known Shannon was depressed, should have looked for signs, should have done something when I looked in on her at 4:00 a.m. on the morning of December 20 and she was breathing funny. I should have listened more, loved more, been a better mother. If only we'd had a better relationship the previous year and all that I had gone through hadn't affected her. If only I'd known about my own depression, maybe I could have seen hers and helped her. If only I had taken her more seriously when she wanted to talk. If only I had seen her pain instead of being so enveloped in my own. If only I'd had a different job that didn't keep me so busy when I was at home. If only I'd listened more and talked less. These and other "if onlys" haunted me for months. The tape played over and over, but never with any answers. There weren't any.

◦℮℮◦

Remorse like this comes with many faces, each unique and streaked with tears. The common denominator is guilt arising from the conviction that you have failed your loved one in some way—if only you had done or not done something, if only you had said or not said something, if only you had known. Guilt is common to the grieving process and can consume anyone who experiences an overwhelming loss.

I (Dave) nearly went insane as a result of the guilt I felt after my three-year-old, Jonathan, died of an undiagnosed illness in 1978. I felt that, as a father, I had failed. The little boy entrusted to me had died, and nothing anybody could say made any real difference.

This image is etched indelibly into the pages of my emotional self: It's the middle of the night and Jonathan is standing on the little stool with his name on it, trying to throw up into the bathroom sink. For three days he's been nauseated, presumably from a viral illness.

"Can I have a drink, Daddy?" he asks.

"Not yet, Jon," I say. "It might make you throw up again."

I didn't know any better. I told him what I'd always heard. How was I supposed to know that the next morning he would experience brain damage from dehydration and, as a result of that, five weeks later he would die?

I, who would have laid down my life defending him against any and all threats, became the means to his death; at least that's the way it felt, and how it felt was all that mattered for months after the event that broke my heart.

Doctors said it wasn't my fault. Friends, family, everybody who knew about it assured me that they wouldn't have handled it differently. I tried to assure myself that I had done the best I knew how. But even if an angel from God had appeared, announcing my absolution, I wouldn't have accepted it.

On one level, I functioned. I had to. There were sermons to preach, classes to teach, weddings and funerals to perform, babies to dedicate, and people to counsel and lead to the Lord. But regardless of how good I became at using my own heartbreak to connect with other people's pain, I couldn't disconnect from my own. I could even help people gain freedom from their own guilt and shame, but I could not set myself free.

Everything I did became another opportunity to be guilty as I pursued myself through the shadowy pathways of my own mind, constantly trying, convicting, and sentencing the villain to the only thing he deserved: torment. If I broke the speed limit, I debated turning myself in. In relation to certain other infractions, I actually did turn myself in, paying one fine. I gradually sank into the quicksand of striving to live as "righteously" as I could, not so much to prove anything as to protect myself from further self-imposed penance. As the real but unresolved guilt I felt about having failed Jonathan attached itself to other things, I became obsessive-compulsive—obsessed with my wrongdoings and compelled to try to release the guilt somehow. I could tell you about the hand washing and the doing, undoing, and doing again that anyone who's been there would recognize.

Perhaps one example will suffice. Early one morning as I drove past a house, the thought hit me that the smoke I saw might be from a fire. I drove a little farther, assuring myself that this was highly unlikely, but then I *had* to go back, to be certain, as much for the good of the people in that house as to protect myself from the possible guilt of not having intervened to save their lives. Even after I was sure it was only chimney smoke, I still had to go back again. And then, after everything was said and done, I chastised myself for not having the willpower to stifle the impression in the first place or to keep myself from returning even when I knew better.

I was probably within an eyelash of insanity as I tried to protect my damaged emotions by not doing any more "bad" things. But no matter what standards I set, I failed, because had I achieved "perfection" for one day—which never happened—I would have chastised myself for setting my standards too low or for taking pride in my achievement, an even more despicable outcome!

The sad fact was I *needed* to fail. Success—any success—would have been too kind an outcome for as negligent a father as I. So I spent a lot of my time apologizing—for actions, inactions, motives, attitudes—because I so desperately needed people telling me I was forgiven. Yet no number of such assurances ever released me from my own emotional prison, designed, constructed, and maintained by a brutal jailer: me.[2]

Well, now you know how I know about the kind of guilt that can hound anyone who has experienced a devastating loss. Whether the guilt is real guilt (feelings of guilt that are related to actual shortcomings) or false guilt (feelings of guilt that are inconsistent with reality) matters little, at least not in the early stages.

Common Guilt-Building Issues for Survivors

We Didn't See It Coming

Jean wrote, "I wonder why I didn't see the signs that Dean was going to kill himself, but now I see them very easily. It breaks my heart that I didn't realize it at the time. I also feel guilty that I didn't go to the court and ask for an injunction from the family members who were hurting Dean so much. I wanted to so badly, but if I had done that, it would have torn our family apart. Now I would do it in a heartbeat, because I would rather have Dean here than worry about having family members upset with me."

Becky said, "We felt guilty because we didn't see that Jason was in any serious trouble that was life-threatening."

We Could Have Done Things Differently

Linda said, "During the first few months, I felt responsible for Paul's death. After all, if I had been a good enough mother, he would have been able to 'do life.' I was also ashamed that he had made the choice to die. I sensed the stigma all around me—some of it was real, some was internally generated."

Florence recalls, "I was overcome with guilt. I would write down what I felt I had done wrong and ask the Lord to forgive me."

Debbie said, "Guilt was a huge obstacle for many months. There will always be a part of me that will question myself on things that I missed with Josh during his bout with depression. I have beaten myself up many times over with things I felt I did wrong and didn't do right with my parenting him."

I (Sue) was plagued by memories of times that I had been a less-than-perfect parent. I would ask myself if that particular incident was the cause of Shannon's decision. I wondered what I could have done differently that could have changed the course of events. This was a continuing question. I blamed myself for her decision.

We Are Blamed or Shamed by Others

Jean was Dean's aunt and legal guardian when he took his life in 2002. Because Dean could not read or write and he was mildly retarded, Jean and her mother managed his money for him. Just prior to his death, Dean had asked for more money from his Social Security disability payment, but Jean had not given it to him because the rent and utilities for Dean's apartment had to be paid soon. As a result, Dean's parents and the extended family blamed Jean for putting the boy over the edge.

"Most of the family members, including my parents, gathered at Dean's parents' the day of the tragedy," Jean said. "There was a verbal battle when my dad heard some of the family members carrying on about it being my fault that Dean did this. I should have given him the money he'd asked for. I should have been there to stop him.

"I wondered: *Are they right? Did I cause Dean to take his life? Was there something I missed? If I hadn't become involved in Dean's life, would he still be here? Maybe I should have just let him have his money and not have worried about whether or not his rent and utilities got paid. Did I push him too hard to be as successful as possible for someone with his disabilities and mental-health issues? Oh, God, what have I done?*

"For several months, many horrible things were said about me and Dean's death being my fault. Each time, the things that were said were more hateful than the time before. The harassing phone calls from Dean's father became so frequent that I had to have his number blocked in order to keep my sanity. I was going into such a deep depression that I suffered insomnia. I stayed up at night to analyze my time with Dean; every day became a struggle. And all the time I wondered, *Was it really my fault?*"

We Survived When Our Loved One Didn't

This is called "survivor guilt," and it is quite common among those who have survived a trauma in which others died. In situations as intense as surviving a loved one's suicide, survivors may convert their intense emotions into a misdirected sense of responsibility and guilt for having survived. Survivor guilt is often compounded by unresolved guilt feelings from as far back as childhood. Differentiating between true guilt and false guilt in such cases can take a long time, even with the help of a competent counselor.

Sometimes those left behind wish it were they who had died. For example, one father signs his email letters: "Robbie Sr. I found my son and cried, but I wish it was I who died! Dad of Robbie — Hanging 8/16/1973 to 12/14/2002."

We Experience a Vicious Cycle of Unexpected Emotions

Linda wrote, "I was angry about everything and with everybody within a few weeks of Paul's suicide. That was mixed with guilt about Paul's choice, embarrassment about the suicide, fear of more loss, heavy sadness about the reality that he was gone, and a touch of relief that the struggle had ended. Feelings of relief were immediately followed by another wave of guilt for feeling relieved!"

Sometimes a survivor's anger, resentment, or disappointment is directed toward the deceased or the medical profession. One man said, "After my wife's death, my son remarked, 'We all failed Mom.' Actually, I feel like she failed us. We tried to get her into counseling over and over again. She was depressed most of the time. The doctor who found her cancer put her on antidepressant medication, which seemed to help her. Another doctor took her off the medication, saying that she didn't need it. A week later she was dead. If the doctors had done as I requested and begged them to do, would she still be here?"

Author Albert Hsu, whose father took his own life, wrote, "Anger is a very common emotion after a suicide. We feel that our loved one's action was utterly selfish, and we are angry at them for leaving us to clean up their mess. Suicide is particularly traumatizing because we do not know how to resolve our hurt and outrage. If it had been a murder, we could grieve for the victim and vent our rage at the murderer. But in the case of suicide, the victim *is* the murderer. And so we are conflicted. We may even hate our loved one for doing this to our loved one. We grieve the suicide and rage against him simultaneously."[3]

Anger like this is usually mixed with guilt for harboring such feelings toward the deceased, and it can be intensified by the reality that forgiveness and reconciliation are no longer options to be pursued, person-to-person. It is common for survivors to feel anger even toward God for allowing the suicide to happen or for not having intervened in some way.

Believers who experience anger toward God usually have their disappointment compounded by the conviction that they should not become upset with the Creator and Sustainer of the universe. This type of guilt can create a sense of distance between the grieving believer and the only true source of comfort, God. Becky said, "I feel guilty because I felt so close to God and felt his presence for the first few months, but I feel like I'm drifting away, and I don't want that." Believers who experience this approach-avoidance conflict in relation to God—wanting to draw near but hindered by negative feelings—will need to be reconciled with him, which is not as easy as uninformed observers may think. The good news is that God will never leave us or forsake us, even when we feel like leaving or forsaking him. Nothing can separate us from his love. Like Francis Thompson's "Hound of Heaven," God will keep seeking us until we understand that the only way to end the hunt is to flee *to* him.

Even when survivors have more positive feelings, such as relief that the problems are finally over or that they are feeling "alive" again, guilt may soon follow because both reactions seem somehow unfair or disloyal to the deceased. When this is the case, the intensity of the guilt may be compounded by the degree of responsibility the survivor feels for what has happened.

I (Dave) was once discussing my lingering sadness over Jonathan's death with a physician, who asked me what I thought I was guilty of.

"Parental malpractice," I replied.

"And what is the sentence?" he asked.

"Lifelong unhappiness" almost instantly sprang from my lips.

A self-imposed sentence like this may sound familiar to survivors of suicide, in which case, it is likely driven by remorse and fueled by the emotional intensity linked to the event, a penance to atone for one's "sin," and is very difficult to resolve without psychological and spiritual counseling.

Grieving the loss of someone you love is no easy journey, for behind every rock or tree along the way lurks a guilt-demon whose only purpose is to drag you back into the slime pit of shame and blame. Such guilt can be incapacitating, but thankfully there is a way beyond it: the grace of God. As the apostle Paul wrote, "Therefore, there is now no condemnation for those who are in Christ Jesus, because through Christ Jesus the law of the Spirit of life set me free from the law of sin and death" (Rom. 8:1–2).

Moving beyond the Guilt

Linda said, "I had to make a conscious decision to stay connected to safe, supportive people. Over time, my support network of several female friends from church helped me work through my guilt and shame by talking about it and sifting through it to determine what was mine and what I needed to let go of."

Louise said, "Guilt has been a huge issue. In the beginning it felt like guilt had a choke hold on me. Through prayer, I have come to realize that I cannot judge what I did back then, with the information I have now. I had no clue my son could be suicidal, and in the beginning I even thought he must have been murdered. I still have a few things I would like to go back and change (one day in particular), but I have worked through the guilt issues. I gave myself permission to be a 'normal parent' and make mistakes with my son, as all parents do. I make them with my daughters also. And I have forgiven myself for those things I did wrong and cannot change. Through prayer, the Lord also showed me that I had actually done a lot more right than I had realized or given myself credit for."

Kathie wrote, "Guilt was there off and on for many years, until I finally realized that Stevie made the decision to kill himself. I had done everything a mother could do to raise a godly child with the materials God gave me from the Scriptures. It really wasn't my fault after all."

Marie wrote, "There has been plenty of guilt. I have dealt with it, and continue to deal with it, by reading my Bible, praying, support groups (many of them), and confession. God is a forgiving God. The hardest thing has been to learn to forgive myself."

FINDING YOUR WAY

Recognize that the guilt you feel can serve as a reminder that, to paraphrase the Westminster Confession of Faith, "You have done some things you ought not to have done, and left undone some things you ought to have done." Further, some feelings of guilt may help you identify unfinished business between you and the deceased or even between you and others still alive.

Connect yourself to safe, supportive people with whom you can share anything without being judged. These people should be spiritually discerning, as you may need help separating real guilt and false guilt. You may then want to ask them to be with you as you confess the real and let go of the false. For example, you might hold a simple ceremony with your friends, in which you burn a list of your false offenses as an offering to the Lord. You might also make a list of the things for which you really are guilty in relation to the deceased. With your friends, go to the gravesite and confess these things with your friends as witnesses. When you're finished, they can represent the Lord and say, "We forgive you."

Diminish the effect of negative thought patterns. Everyone has some regrets; some people have many. But your regrets need not control all your waking thoughts, draining energy that could be employed in pursuing wholeness. Since the mind can only dwell on one thing at a time, if you fill your mind with good and wholesome things, these thoughts can over time replace the older, more negative connections.[4]

Acknowledge that your inner conflict is spiritual in nature. It mirrors the ongoing battle between God, who is for you, and Satan, who is your accuser (in Hebrew, *Satan* means "accuser"). Revelation 12:10 celebrates Satan's ultimate demise: "Now have come the salvation and the power and the kingdom of our God, and the authority of his Christ. For the accuser of our brothers, who accuses them before our God day and night, has been hurled down." The scenario here has four parties: God, Jesus, Satan, and believers, whom Satan is accusing, something like this: "How can so-and-so be a believer, when he does this and that?" Jesus, whom the Bible describes as our advocate (defense attorney), steps up and says, "Yes, so-and-so has done this and that, but my death atoned for it all. There is therefore no condemnation for him. He is forgiven."

Use spiritual means to fight spiritual battles. The apostle Paul, who knew a lot about spiritual warfare, described "dressing for battle" in the truth of God's Word and then standing on that truth to defeat the enemy. "Be strong in the Lord and in his mighty power. Put on the full armor of God so that you can take your stand against the devil's schemes. For our struggle is not against flesh and blood, but against the rulers, against the authorities, against the powers of this dark world and against the spiritual forces of evil in the heavenly realms. Therefore put on the full armor of God, so that when the day of evil comes, you may be able to stand your ground, and after you have done everything, to stand" (Eph. 6:10–13).

Practice spiritual judo. Use the moves of your opponent (Satan) against him, as in judo. When you are tempted to focus on your guilt, real or false, you could stop and pray for someone; anyone will do. Since the power of prayer is one thing the accuser fears, the more you employ this strategy, the less he will harass you.

Record your thoughts and feelings in a journal. Many survivors have found that journaling has helped them, over time, to sort out how they really feel and what they really think about what has happened. If you choose to keep a journal, you might consider ending each entry with a prayer that begins

"Lord, thank you . . ." Sometimes it may be difficult to identify *anything* for which you are thankful, but if you search your mind and heart, you'll find something, even if it's only "Lord, thank you that you are making this journey with me." When you review your notes later, you'll be amazed at the depth of your struggle but also encouraged by the progress you've made.

Be aware that things may get worse before they get better. Some survivors have found that while the first few months of the journey are difficult enough, sometime between four and six months after the death of their loved one, they come up against a wall called reality. The shock has worn off, the emotions are less intense, and the realization sets in that the deceased will never come home again. We'll address this phase of the journey in the next chapter.

I Cannot Make It on My Own

I come to you, my Father, so grateful you are here
When the times seem so unbearable, yet I cannot shed a tear.
The pain runs deep and lingers, so near and yet so far
And my one and only comfort is to come to where you are.
My only son was buried a year ago this day,
I do not understand it—I don't want to hurt this way.
I come to you so boldly, for I know you know my pain.
I lean on you, for it's your strength that helps me to sustain.
Tell me please, my Father, as your son died that day,
Did you turn your face in anguish—is that why you looked away?
My son is all around me, yet he's nowhere to be found
For memories linger everywhere, but he is not around.
I know he walks in meadows far beyond what I could dream,
A place where all the earthly cares give way to things serene.
His heart's no longer heavy with a weight too large to bear,
And now, at last, he finally knows how much we really care.
And so I've come to ask of you, this prayer that fills my heart,
As holidays approach this year and merriment seems tart.
Father, walk me day by day, to that place we'll meet again,
For I cannot make it on my own, I need to hold your hand.

—LOUISE WIRICK[1]

CHAPTER 4

The Wall

T. S. Eliot wrote, "Humankind cannot bear very much reality," a statement that applies in a special sense to survivors of suicide. For adjusting to what has happened requires facing reality, which can seem like a wall you've crashed up against. Because we all grieve uniquely, your encounter with the wall may happen at any time, though it usually occurs between three and six months into the grieving process. Knowing it will happen may help you avoid being broken by the impact.

In his book *Life after Loss*, Bob Deits writes, "The third month after the loss of a loved one is often one of the most difficult times of all. By then all vestiges of shock and numbness are gone and the full impact of the loss is upon you. Enough has happened by this time that denying your loss is impossible. The difficult adjustments of this step along the way to recovery will go on for some time."[2]

Louise stated that she battled with suicidal thoughts around three months after her son's death. "If I had not had the Lord to lean on," she said, "I have no doubt that I would not have survived my son's death."

For me (Sue), reality hit with a vengeance about four months after Shannon died. I just didn't think I could go on any longer. I realized I would never see her again in this life, and I couldn't imagine living five, ten, or fifteen years without her.

Monica said, "The wall was at the three-month period for me. The shock had finally worn off, and it just hit me like a ton of bricks: *Oh my God, he is really gone.* I still feel that horrible disbelief every now and then. Most days, I

47

cope. I know he isn't here anymore. But there are days that I have to shake myself mentally. It's like the wind has been knocked out of me, I can't breathe, and I think, *My baby brother is not ever coming back.* And then I cry. And I may cry for days. Then I buck up, and things go back to 'normal.'

"But then it happens again. It never really goes away. It's always there under the surface, and at any moment it hits again. It's like standing in the ocean; it may be calm for a while, and then a boat may ride by, and wave after wave hits you until it calms down again. Well, that's how grief is for me. At six months, at nine months, and so on. Sometimes I don't think the waves will ever stop. I know that boat will always drive by and break the calm until I am gone too."

"*Wall* is an appropriate term!" Terri said. "In the same week I turned thirty — now that seems quite small in the big picture — Jack, my fiancé, took his own life. He was six years older than me, so he affectionately called me 'Little One' or 'Baby.' He had promised me an 'over-the-hill' party when I turned thirty, but he wasn't here to fulfill that obligation.

"At six months, I thought I was doing well even though I was just going through the motions of life. Then shock and numbness wore off, and reality *hurt!* In my case, a couple of reality checks occurred at this interval. A thirteen-year-old boy who attended my daughter's school took his own life. I came out of the shell of my own grief to talk with my daughter about depression, choices, and the resources available to her — teachers, counselors, pastor, and family — should she ever need to talk to anyone.

"My family came to my rescue. I'm adopted and came home from the hospital when I was eight days old. This year we chose to postpone my birthday and to celebrate instead thirty years of my being part of the family. It was much easier for me to feel happiness on the anniversary of my homecoming rather than on my actual birthday.

"The wall is the time when everyone around you feels they have given you enough time to 'get over it' and move on with life," Terri added. "A male friend offered to take me to a movie. We were totally unaware that halfway through the feature one character would put a pistol in his mouth and pull the trigger. I ran out of the theater in hysterics. The manager and my friend found me crying on the curb. After that, I asked my friends to prescreen movies before I would see them."

Elements of the Wall

For survivors of suicide, there are at least eight "stones" in the wall called reality. Each must be dealt with or resolved for your progress to continue. As you progress, keep in mind the spiral staircase we described earlier, since you may not always move from point to point, but rather it may sometimes seem that you are going in circles.

Stone 1: You will never see that loved one again in this life. Ginger described how it affected her: "For us the first year of all the holidays and Todd's birthday (which was only a little over five weeks after he died) and his death anniversary were extremely hard on us," she wrote. "The days leading up to each special day were filled with apprehension and a lot of anxiety, more so than the actual day itself. It's like you want to run and hide, to skip right over the day, ignore it in any way you can.

"Christmas is one of the worst holidays, since it's hard to ignore when the celebrations and decorations are all around you. And it's such a family time, and you don't have yours. I still to this day look at whole, complete families around Christmastime and think, *We used to be just like that.* And then the loneliness grips my heart.

"The first year of everything is somewhat worse because you don't know what to expect. You don't know if you're going to actually get through it or just die from a broken heart. But for me, the second, and the third, and the fourth years were similar in heartache and loneliness, because no matter what, our family will never be again. We'll never know the joys of sharing again.

"I started seeing a female psychologist very shortly after Todd's death, and she told me I would start feeling worse at the 'six-month hump' (her words exactly). I couldn't believe what she was telling me. 'How in the world could I feel any worse than I do now?' I asked. She said, 'About then, the realization will set in that Todd will *never* be coming back. And knowing that, you will start to question yourself about what color his eyes were, how his laugh sounded, what he smelled like, things like that.'

"At the time, I thought she was totally nuts, but she was right. At right around six months, I couldn't play the mind games—*He's on vacation. I've just seen him. He's fine. He's going to call me soon*—any more. And sometimes I would squeeze my eyes shut so tightly, trying to remember every little detail about Todd, that I would end up with a terrific headache. And I got very angry with myself and felt guilty, because there were times when my memory of Todd was not clear. I questioned my sanity, asking myself, *Did he ever really exist? Was I really his mom?*

"It was right around the six-month mark that I was put on medication to calm my nerves. That slight bit of hope I had held for months—that this was all just a bad nightmare—was gone. And almost everyone around me, who had supported me and my husband, were now back to their own world, leaving me more lonely and distraught. I literally thought I would die from the pain in my own heart.

"This turmoil lasted until I made it past Todd's death anniversary. And although the antidepressant did help me to slow down the horrible thoughts in my head, after about seven to eight months of taking them, I stopped, because I knew that no matter what, they could not change what had happened."

Stone 2: Painful reminders are everywhere. These can appear out of nowhere and are often lurking around every corner ready to pounce and knock the wind out of you all over again. You hear your song, the one that was playing when you promised to love each other forever and life seemed so right. You can't bear to look at your photo album, but to hide it away feels almost like an affront to the deceased. The personal belongings of your loved one are constant reminders of what *was*, while silently screaming at you to deal with what *is*. Sights, sounds, smells, and places all serve as reminders of that person you loved and lost.

While rewinding the tape and clearing messages on my answering machine four months after Shannon died, I (Sue) came across a message from her that had been left on the tape the previous June—six months before she died. The emotional struggle after hearing her voice was long and painful.

The difficulty with such reminders is that they keep the pain of reality "in your face." The reminders are everywhere, and they come when least expected. They are like guests who show up at a fancy dinner party wearing beach attire; they just don't fit into your plans. Eventually, however, you may come to see the blessings in these reminders, in spite of the pain they evoke. They serve to keep the memory of your loved one alive. One of the fears that many survivors experience is that the loved one will be forgotten, that memories of how they looked, what they sounded like, or what they smelled like will fade with time.

Stone 3: Holidays, birthdays, and other anniversaries intensify your grief. These dates, which may have held special meaning for you in the past, may now become dates you would prefer to skip over or sleep through. New dates are now added to your calendar. You will remember the day he died, the day she would have turned forty, the day he would have graduated from medical school, dates with a meaning that you never intended.

Holidays and other special occasions become especially difficult because happy memories of past celebrations become clouded with the pain and tears shed over this year's celebration. What once brought you joy may now become a burden you just don't want to carry.

Stone 4: Your grief may be compounded by other losses. A suicide may come at a time when you are grieving other losses or are involved in dealing with other major issues. For me (Sue), Shannon's suicide came after a year of losses piled on top of one another. I had a job loss due to the bankruptcy of the company I was working for, a change to another company and all that entailed, a loss of financial stability, a major health scare (possible breast cancer; biopsy normal), the hospitalization of a family member, and then Shannon's suicide. There wasn't time after each situation to adequately deal with that loss before the next one hit. Two months after Shannon died, my former mother-in-law died. The net effect was staggering.

Stone 5: Your sense of loss will intensify when you ponder what might have been. Debbie described this dynamic in relation to her son: "I see all that he is missing out on. His siblings are growing up and doing things now that he will never have the chance to do. He should be here to experience it all with them. He should be here now, at almost twenty-two years of age, possibly married, possibly a parent himself. He should know his cousins and watch them grow. I should have been able to watch him drive his first car, help him get ready for his first prom, watch him walk down to get his diploma, watch him take his vows with his wife, stand next to him while he helps birth his children. There are things I didn't get to do and will never get to do with Josh."

If you have lost your spouse or fiancé, it means the loss of the intimate love relationship you shared; the loss of future plans and dreams; the loss of seeing your children grow up, get married, and give you grandchildren; often the loss of financial stability; and the loss of social relationships. You are thrown into aloneness, leaving only you to deal with all the things once shared with your partner.

Stone 6: You may be disappointed, abandoned, or criticized — compounding your pain. These disappointments are especially difficult when they are caused by people whom you expected would support you. You may be surprised and dismayed to learn that others share your ambivalent feelings about the suicide of your loved one.

Some people may say and do hurtful things out of ignorance. They don't know what to say or do. They may feel awkward and not know how to help you. Such people, in the long run, are easier to forgive than are the critics and judges.

Some people may suggest failure on your part, implying that you are somehow responsible for your loved one's actions. Such statements are likely to compound your anger and sense of distance from those critics, from whom you will pull away. To add insult to injury, the same critics may then criticize you for pulling away, as if you have an obligation to endure their drivel.

Because of the nature of suicide and the myths and misunderstanding surrounding it, you may feel stigmatized to some degree. Friends and others who once were supportive may now avoid you because they feel that someone they know and love may follow your loved one's example. They may feel (or even say) there is something wrong with you and your family because normal people don't take their own lives.

People who were initially supportive will eventually return to their own lives, expecting that you will return to yours in a relatively (often unreasonably) short amount of time, that you will "get over it" and move on. What they don't realize is that you can't really get over it because your life is permanently altered and you've become immersed in a search for a new normal, which no one else can define for you.

Stone 7: You may experience a variety of disturbing emotional symptoms. Common among these symptoms are flashbacks, anxiety and panic attacks, agitation and angry outbursts, suicidal thoughts, nightmares, feeling the presence of your loved one, hearing her voice, smelling her particular scent, thinking you've just seen her on the street or in the mall. When you experience these sensations, you may think you are losing your mind.

Stone 8: You may experience new and disturbing physical symptoms. Studies of bereaved parents indicate that about 25 percent experience diminished
natural immunity around the sixth month after a major loss.[3] To our knowledge, no similar studies have been done with survivors of suicide, but logic suggests that during this period of your grief recovery, you may be more vulnerable
to contagious diseases and allergies.

I (Sue) found myself constantly battling colds and the more severe symptoms of bronchitis the winter after Shannon died. Normal spring allergies
turned into one sinus infection after another. Other survivors have reported that
physical symptoms and diseases they had before their loss intensified afterward.
In addition, as we've mentioned earlier, some new physical symptoms may
accompany depression, complicating proper diagnosis and treatment.

FINDING YOUR WAY

**When the fact that you will never see your loved one
again has you down,** try to harness and redirect your intense
emotional energy in a constructive direction. For example, as
a holiday approaches, you might think of ways to honor your
memory of the deceased. If he cared about the poor, at Christmas you might "adopt" a needy family and give them gifts from
your loved one.

If you find yourself stuck at "If only she were here," you
might ask what charitable act she would do if she were here,
and then go and do that kindness in her name.

Or if you are mired in loneliness, you might spend the day
with someone you know to be lonely. The principal here is to
identify the need, wish, or yearning that is the source of your
own pain, and then turn that pain on its head by trying to
meet that need in someone else's life.

When painful memories ambush you, seek ways to turn the
pain into thanksgiving. For example, it's likely that for a long
time after your loved one's death, your primary emotion when

he comes to mind will be pain—nameless, beyond control pain. But at some point, when these memories come, you will begin to be thankful that you knew him at all. That's the way it was for me (Dave) after Jonathan died. It took a long time, longer than anyone expected, but finally I could say I was thankful that I had known him, if only for a little while.

When you face anniversaries, especially the first ones, try to prepare yourself. Judy T. wrote, "Lea died in August, so when Thanksgiving came, we were still stumbling in the dark. So we went to dinner with the same people we had eaten Thanksgiving dinner with for the prior four years. It was the safest thing to do. At Christmas, I called up some of the many people who gave the vague frustrating offer 'If there is anything I can do' and took them up on it. I made a pot of chili and people brought stuff, I got out our decorations, and we decorated and really had fun. We hung up all the stockings early, and all of us at one time or another wrote a note and put it in Lea's stocking. This has become an annual event. Notes still get added, after six years. I don't know about anyone else, but I haven't read them yet. Perhaps someday I will.

"In terms of anniversaries and birthdays," she added, "the ones we planned for went fine. The ones we tried to skip were awful. Each year we plan less and less and it is okay, but we still mark the days."

Linda told us, "These are what I call 'in my face' times—times that magnify the grief experience with intensified reminders of my loss. Paul died in June, so I was blessed with a few months to prepare for my first holidays after his suicide. I had time to study and plan for what I knew would be a difficult season. Though the dense fog of shock was beginning to lift by October, I experienced the holidays on automatic pilot—with as much healthy self-care as I could muster. Family dinners usually held at my house were farmed out to others. Decorations were kept to a minimum. And time was allowed (and permission given) for the inevitable tears, guilt, and anger.

"Every room in my house had its own tissue box for at least the first year. As difficult as Thanksgiving and Christmas were, the first birthday and first Mother's Day after Paul's suicide were much worse," Linda continued. "I planned diligently for the first anniversary of his death and expected to wake up that day and be done with the grieving process. Much to my surprise (and dismay), I spent another year or two working through the acute pain, guilt, and anger of my loss.

"My sense is that holidays and anniversaries are difficult for survivors because these occasions are supposed to be celebrated with joy, and our joy is buried deep beneath the rubble of suicide grief for what seems to be a very long time. After ten

REFLECTIONS OF A SURVIVOR

The Glass Door

At the end of my yearlong tunnel of grieving, I can see—through my tears—a radiant glass door. On June 29, 1994, I plan to open that door, walk through it, and close it behind me.

For the rest of my life, I will be able to look back and see through the clear glass to the memories of these past twelve months, but I choose not to open the door again and return down that hall of intense emotions and difficult decisions. All of the painful first anniversary dates will be behind the door: the first Thanksgiving and Christmas, the first birthday, the first Mother's Day, and finally, the first anniversary of Paul's death. I choose to make the second anniversaries somewhat easier.

As I walk through the glass door at the end of the hall, I face a future that is bright with a heart that is full. Though the pain of my son's suicide will always be a part of me, it is diminishing. It is being replaced daily with the love of a comforting God and my faithful friends and family. They have steadfastly shared my journey to the glass door, and I trust them to continue to be with me on the other side of it. For all of that, I am truly grateful.

So, I soon face an anniversary—and a victory.

I made it through the first year!

—LINDA L. FLATT, MAY 1994

years, divine provision, a lot of grief work, and loving support from others, I have reclaimed my joy and now am able to participate in family celebrations, holidays, and anniversaries without being overwhelmingly reminded of my loss. Though Paul is not physically present at these gatherings, I can celebrate his life without being crushed by sadness. There will always be a remnant of pain, but it no longer overshadows my joy."[4]

If you have faced multiple losses, don't go it alone. Maybe after the first disaster happened, you just hung in there, trying to survive a cauldron of reactions and emotions you never imagined possible. *Survive* is a key word in the preceding sentence, for people who don't understand the depth of your grief use words like "deal with," "overcome," "rise above," or "conquer," when you were just hoping that if you held on long enough, you would, in a sense, get beyond it. But the suicide did not add to your burden; it *multiplied* it.

You need to put aside all thought of trying to be strong, resilient, able to bounce back, and all the other unrealistic expectations of yourself, and let yourself be helped. This means letting someone else inside your pain; and choosing who that might be is scary, for sure. But if you insist on proving something to yourself or others by going it alone, you may find yourself fighting on too many fronts at once. Grief related to multiple losses can become quite complicated, frightening, even deadly—emotionally, physically, spiritually, and relationally. Because of this, you need to enlist allies who are qualified to help. These are usually, but not always, professionals.

If you had unresolved issues with the deceased, you can't change the issues but you can change the way you relate to them. If there are regrets, you can resolve them over time, though it will require some hard work and probably more time than you might wish. Resolving issues when a person is gone is different from, but still similar to, the process required when a person is alive. Forgiveness and reconciliation can take place, usually with the help of an understanding friend or counselor who might take the place of the loved one and engage you in a healing conversation related to the event(s) in question. Certain Christian counseling techniques specialize in this type of inner healing or healing of memories.

In terms of your present sense of loss, the emptiness and frustration you feel because your loved one is no longer present can be extreme, especially during the first year. Your best approach is to face these feelings realistically, realizing that the intensity of your pain is an indicator of the depth of your love. The truth is that only God can fill this void with his love. Yet more amazing is that he is willing to do so.

If you experience rejection from some people, others will still be there for you, letting you talk as much as you need to and listening without judgment. Do not hesitate to limit your time and energy to these dear friends. Carefully choose those with whom you share the details of your loved one's death, in part because of the difficulty of explaining things to people who can't or won't understand. Setting boundaries around your fragile emotions is a good idea. As you heal and the loss of your loved one becomes less painful, you may decide to share the loss with more people. This decision and its timing are choices only you can make.

If you think you've lost your mind, don't despair. Just the fact that you worry about this is evidence that you are still sane. Many survivors of devastating losses experience disturbing symptoms, though they may not often discuss them. These symptoms include thinking you have seen, heard, or smelled your deceased loved one or that you've sensed that he or she is right there with you. Often these sensations happen at night, in the quiet darkness when you long for that person to be there with you. You may replay over and over the details of the days or hours leading up to the suicide. These and other similar psychological phenomena are your mind's way of processing what has happened, while protecting you from the raw force of the pain. You can move with this process by pondering what the most disturbing symptoms may indicate, including whether there remain unresolved issues with the deceased.

With time and the establishment of a new normal, most symptoms of this type will diminish in intensity and frequency. You could expedite this process by meeting with a counselor experienced in working with survivors of suicide. A trustworthy friend could help by listening and loving you through this time, but usually such deeply personal matters are best entrusted to a medical, psychological, or pastoral professional.

If you experience an array of new and disturbing physical symptoms, realize that this is your body's way of expressing the intensity of your sense of loss. It is crucial to take care of yourself physically during this period, including eating the right foods—which may be difficult because comfort foods are often not very nutritious—getting sufficient rest, exercising in moderation, and being careful about the use of alcohol or drugs, including prescription drugs.

We suggest you see your doctor as a preventive measure if you have any new physical symptoms. Be frank about what is happening and seek advice regarding health-promoting strategies you might employ, including the use of nutritional supplements and other natural remedies.[4] If the doctor feels you are experiencing depression, cooperate with the treatment plan and be grateful for the wide variety of pharmaceutical and other treatments that exist today, as compared to only a few years ago when people experiencing similar distress were more or less on their own to cope as well as they could.

When you're ready, you will most likely find it helpful to your physical and emotional health to become part of a supportive network of people, such as a grief-recovery group and/or a survivors-of-suicide support group.

SURVIVING THE HOLIDAYS AFTER THE LOSS OF A LOVED ONE

Shortly after my son's suicide in 1993, a wise counselor told me not to let that death take away my joy. At the time, those words fell on deaf ears. But as the days passed and healing began, his guidance became my mission—to somehow reclaim my joy after experiencing the incomprehensible suicide death of my child. The powerful and overwhelming emotions that embody the grieving process tend to be magnified during the holidays—a time when memories of our missing loved ones are especially painful.

Family gatherings are wearying reminders of the stark reality of our loss. Here are some steps we can take together to endeavor to recover our God-given joy during a difficult holiday season.

Decide to prepare. Plan ahead for the pitfalls of holiday bereavement. Educate yourself in the fine art of surviving the holidays and equip yourself for the season. Beware of the expectations of others and choose to get through the holidays your way!

Determine to feel. Give yourself permission to grieve during the holidays instead of "stuffing" or denying your emotions. Resist the urge to shut down emotionally until next year. Trust me, the feelings will still be on that shelf on January 1, and they will, more than likely, be even more powerful and destructive than they were in December if you take that route.

Commit to connect. Choose to be around safe, supportive people during the holidays—people who will let you have your grief. Make a conscious decision to stay connected to God and his people at a time when you may want to isolate yourself to ease your pain. We serve a loving, comforting God, and there is great healing in his community. Reach out and take the light and love that others offer during the holidays—and, in turn, give whatever you can to those who reach out to you.

—LINDA L. FLATT, NOVEMBER 1998

The Agony of Grief

The agony of grief comes like a thief in the night.
Your emotions are torn and wound up tight.
The happiness is replaced as despair sets in.
You retreat into a shell deep inside your skin.
Everyday occurrences seem to annoy.
Life is different, you find it hard to enjoy.
Shock and disbelief are taking their toll,
Reaching right in to your very soul.
You have nowhere to run, nowhere to go.
Your world is turned inside out—it has to show.
Life for you changed instantly that day.
You only wish you could make it go away.
Anger, denial, and vengeance come over you.
The answers you look for just won't do.
The road of grief is hard yet long.
That is when you must be strong.
The agony of grief that comes in the night
Will fade away one day and be out of sight.

—ROBERT WALTERS SR.[1]

CHAPTER 5

Depression, the Scourge of Broken Hearts

The pious-platitude sign in front of a certain evangelical protestant church declared, "WE ARE TOO BLESSED TO BE DEPRESSED." Most likely, some who attend this church were pleased with this statement, while others realized it was just another uninformed religious pseudo-poet's declaration that people of faith — in this case, enough faith to recall their blessings — will never experience depression.

With such beliefs common in the church, is it any wonder that believers who are depressed often feel misunderstood, judged, or rejected by their Christian friends? For a person whose depression follows the suicide of a loved one, this kind of treatment from brothers and sisters whose support the survivor desperately need adds a new measure of pain to the pain she already carries.

Depression in Survivors of Suicide

Depression is a not a state of mind; it is a state marked by a sense of being pressed down, weighed down, or burdened. Depression is much more than a set of medical symptoms. It is a multifaceted disorder affecting every aspect of a person's life — physical, mental, relational, and spiritual.

Most survivors of suicide experience depression to one degree or another following the death of their loved one. This is a normal component of the grieving process and a reasonable response to what has happened. With time, the support of loved ones, and perhaps some counseling, this kind of depression usually diminishes.

Some survivors, however, develop major depression, which is also called "clinical depression" because it is usually diagnosed in a clinical setting such as a hospital or a physician's office. This chapter is written especially for survivors with clinical depression and those who want to understand and help them.

The diagnosis of major depression is not as simple as the diagnosis of other maladies such as diabetes or pneumonia, which display some quantifiable scientific evidence of the disease. The diagnosis of major depression is based on the presence and duration of symptoms that can vary in intensity—specifically, when five or more of the symptoms listed below have been present for two weeks or longer and are significantly interfering with a person's ability to function in social settings, including in marriage and family relationships and in the workplace. The symptoms of major depression include:

- Persistent sadness, unhappiness, or irritability
- Lethargy or fatigue
- Loss of interest in previously enjoyable activities
- Sudden change in appetite (either more or less)
- Disruption of normal sleep patterns
- Feeling guilty or worthless
- Moving about more slowly and sluggishly, or feeling restless and needing to move all of the time
- Difficulty thinking or concentrating
- Recurrent thoughts of suicide or death

If five or more of these symptoms describe your current patterns of thought or emotion, have persisted for two weeks or longer, and are interfering with your day-to-day functioning at home or at work, please see a physician right away. While your symptoms may be caused by an underlying illness other than depression, a battery of tests will help you and your doctor rule this out before pursuing treatment for the most likely cause, considering your history with suicide. In terms of your history, be sure to tell the doctor all that has happened and the changes that have occurred—physically, emotionally, relationally, and spiritually. (For a brief depression self-check, see appendix 1.)

Ginger describes how it has been for her since her son, Todd, took his own life on July 27, 1994: "Not one day has passed since then that I have not dealt with depression and utter loneliness. I can start a morning bright and optimistic, but no matter how I try, in the early afternoon I become withdrawn, very tired, with a total feeling of defeat. I can be with a group of people, working, alone, on vacation, busy doing something around the house, at the grocery store—it does not matter—the depression and sadness hit me around 1:00 p.m. I just drag through it, try to change my mindset, but nothing works. So I have become resigned to it. Around dusk it usually starts to dissipate because I know that soon I won't be able to see the little soft white puffy clouds in an otherwise sunny sky . . . like the day Todd died."

Many survivors with clinical depression are tempted to deny they need medical help—as in, "I'm okay. This isn't that serious." Or if someone who cares about them suggests that a medical evaluation is warranted, they respond, "Why won't people just leave me alone? I don't need to see a doctor for this. I just need to have things the way they were before."

Some survivors struggle so hard for so long with their loss that they cannot discern when they have moved beyond normal grieving into something a lot more serious. "In Jason's suicide note," wrote Becky, survivor since October 2002, "he wanted me to 'grieve for a little while and then laugh and be happy.' I've been trying to put depression at the back of my mind and convince myself that I was just grieving. But I've had many of the typical symptoms—not sleeping, ulcer acting up, not being interested in anything anymore, not eating, not caring whether I lived or died, basically willing myself to die and feeling so empty inside."

Some survivors may not see the degree of their depression until years later. "I had never suffered any type of depression until Josh died," wrote Debbie, survivor since November 1996. "Afterward, I would sit in my corner of the couch each morning—sometimes I had lain there all night because I couldn't sleep—but I would just sit there, motionless, thinking, rehashing Josh's and my last conversations, looking for answers to why. Now I realize this was depression. It didn't matter if I ate or not, if I slept or not. I didn't leave the house unless I had to go pick up my surviving children. It didn't matter to me. All along, I remember thinking: *If I feel this bad now, how awful it must have been for my son. He must have felt a hundred times worse than me because he chose death.*"

No doubt you noted in these personal stories the various symptoms of major depression that we listed earlier, some of which were mentioned by the survivors quoted above. All of these survivors are recovering today, thanks in part to the excellent antidepressant medications that have become available within the past twenty years or so.

Tricyclic antidepressant medications such as imipramine were first introduced in the late 1940s. These were followed by other antidepressants in the 1970s and early 1980s. But the really effective medications, starting with Prozac, first appeared in 1988.

For some whose journey with surviving depression began much earlier, however, depression and other expressions of mental illness have been nearly lifelong companions. "My mother killed herself when I was eight," Lucy, a survivor since 1961, wrote. "My depression was caused by a lot of pent-up anger and frustration that would occasionally break through. I never hurt anyone, but I did a lot of yelling that I regret. I also went from being a star athlete to an obese woman by age thirty-four. Finally, at age fifty, when I had my second massive nervous breakdown (the other was at age twenty), I discovered the value of a really good therapist, antidepressant drugs, exercise, a healthful diet, keeping a personal journal, and maintaining a healthy balance between work and play."

Treatments for Depression

Because depression is a multifaceted condition — we prefer to call it a bio-psycho-socio-spiritual disorder — the most effective treatment for depression involves a team approach, as Lucy described. Medication, counseling, exercise, improved nutrition, journaling, maintaining a balance between work and play, spiritual support, and experiencing the support of a group are all components of a good health-recovery plan.

But since the most common component of major depression is the depletion of chemicals, called neurotransmitters, in the brain, the first line of treatment for major depression should be medical. The right medication or combination of medications at the right dose, used for a long-enough period of time, will help most people with depression improve, providing a solid foundation for rebuilding their broken world.

Antidepressants are the primary medical treatment for depression. These medications are not uppers or stimulants, from which you just come down again and which can be addictive because as time goes on, you will need more of them to achieve the same effect.

Certain chemicals transmit signals between brain cells, which are called neurons. These chemicals are called neurotransmitters. Many people with depression have less than the normal amount of the neurotransmitter serotonin, which relates to one's sense of well-being. The most common antidepressants (for example, Prozac, Zoloft, Lexapro) help to gradually restore the brain's chemical balance by blocking the absorption of serotonin, which is why these medications are called selective serotonin reuptake inhibitors (SSRIs). SSRIs do not turn you into a zombie, on a constant high and out of control; they restore your ability to be yourself. This will enable you to more effectively pursue the rest of your treatment plan, which should include counseling and spiritual support.

I (Sue) was in such a fog and confused, angry, and not thinking clearly when I was in major depression that my relationship with the Lord also suffered. It was only *after* I started the medications and my mind started clearing that I could focus on God as well as on other relationships. My view of antidepressants is that they don't take away your problems; they just help you cope with them better.

More than twenty antidepressants are currently available, with new ones being regularly released.[2] Not all are SSRIs, because SSRIs do not work for everyone. In fact, though your doctor may prescribe an SSRI to start, no one can predict which medication or combination of medications and at what dosage will be most effective in any specific case. It is crucial to work closely with your doctor until you have found the most effective treatment for you.

In my case (Dave), it took about a year to determine the right medication and dosage for me. But once we got it right, I felt like Dante's famous traveler who, having emerged from his journey to the lower realms, said: "And so we came forth, and once again beheld the stars."[3] In fact, as I write this line, I am camped under the stars near Chair Mountain, Colorado. When I was suffering from major depression, I didn't know, nor did I care, if any stars were still up there.

Counseling for Depression

A combination of good medical treatment and "talk therapy" will effectively treat major depression in most cases. The method used by a particular counselor will reflect the counselor's training and experience plus his or her understanding of reality—for example, whether or not the counselor believes that human beings have souls and believes there really is a God to whom all must answer and upon whom the existence of all things depends.

If the counselor believes that you need behavioral retraining, he will try to reinforce behavior that will alleviate depression or help you extinguish behavior that increases depression. If the therapist believes that repressed anger or grudges cause most depression, she will try to help you bring these out in the open so you can resolve them. If the counselor believes that sin or guilt causes depression, he is going to try to help you deal with these issues. Or if the therapist believes that religion is a primary cause for depression, you can expect to be urged to view religion negatively. Since there are as many counseling methods as there are counselors, it is absolutely reasonable to inquire about the counselor's views before beginning therapy.

The most effective counseling for a survivor with depression will match the individual's issues or needs, without violating her belief system. It will also connect the survivor with hope—hope that there really is a reason to embrace life again, painful as it can be, and leave the slow dying called depression behind.

Be Prepared

To our knowledge, there is no scientific evidence that suicide survivors are more at risk for major depression than is the general population, for which the prevalence runs from 5 to 10 percent. But since your loved one who died by suicide was most likely depressed and a tendency toward depression sometimes runs in families, it is wise to watch (and have others help you watch) for depression's symptoms in your life. You can use the list already cited, or you could use the Depression Self-Check in appendix 1 to evaluate your current status. As you do so, keep in mind that most people with clinical depression are not as aware of the degree of their depression as others close to them might be, so having someone help you answer the questions as accurately as possible is not a bad idea.

Over time, you can compare your responses to the Depression Self-Check to chart your progress. I (Dave) have found this simple self-test helpful over the past couple of years as a depression "thermometer." Thankfully, though my score was sometimes as high as seven, today it's within normal limits, for reasons I'll describe later in this chapter.

For survivors, symptoms of clinical depression may find expression at any time but will most likely appear between the third and twelfth months of your journey, as described by the following survivors as they reflected on their own journey.

Louise wrote, "Sometime around the third month, I felt like the depth of my loss suddenly snuck up from behind me and had a choke hold on me. For me (and many others I have helped through that first year), it was worse than the week my son died. I was scared, so I called Hospice and told them it felt like I was getting worse instead of better. The pain, the despair, the inability to think, focus, or connect thoughts—I couldn't seem to concentrate for even a minute! I thought I had gone over the edge and that it was permanent. I was sure I was getting worse day by day. I fought suicidal thoughts during this time because the pain felt so much bigger than me. Had it not been for clinging to God, I don't think I'd be here today. Thank God for being a loving Father!

"Then around the seventh to eighth month, there was a slump. It seemed like I was beginning to do better and I felt like it *might* be possible to get through this—and then *bam!* Out of nowhere, with no warning, I felt like a huge wave knocked me on my butt, and I couldn't figure out why I had suddenly regressed. I felt like I just woke up one morning and everything had changed on me. I struggled to believe I could survive this, and every baby step I took in the healing process seemed to come with much more concentrated effort and prayer. I was still taking those baby steps, but it felt like I was wearing lead shoes.

"Then that one-year mark hit me. Actually, it started in the eleventh month. The days leading up to a Tender Day—that's what we call anniversary dates, birthdays, and so on—are usually worse than the actual day. This was when I fought suicidal thoughts the most. I felt like my cycle of pain (the preceding year) would continue year after year, and that was what I would call 'life' from now on."

Beware the Death Wish

Becky wrote, "In the first few weeks after Jason's suicide, I thought about suicide a lot. I wanted to be with my son. I couldn't see any way of getting past the disaster that had struck our family. The thing that was stopping me was deciding how to do the suicide. I didn't want my family to hurt the way I hurt when I found my son, so a gun was out of the question. I thought about pills but figured I'd probably just throw up and wouldn't die anyway. Turn the car on in the closed garage — maybe. I can't honestly say the thoughts don't still go through my head, but I'm pretty sure I wouldn't have the courage to go through with it."

We think it is more than likely that most survivors will at least consider ending their pain in one way or another. We mention this not to frighten you but to encourage you, if you are thinking this way, to tell someone — physician, support group, pastor, friend — anyone to whom such thoughts can be entrusted. Be prepared to answer some specific questions, including: "How serious are these inclinations, and how long have you had them?" "Do you have a plan as to how and when you might do this?" "Would you like help in protecting you from yourself?"

To take this unexpected fallout for survivors one step further, while some may be tempted to actually kill themselves, many others will be tempted to destroy themselves in one way or another — their reputation via some uncharacteristic act, their financial security via risky ventures, their marriage via infidelity, their reliability and productivity via the use of alcohol or drugs. These too are all efforts to mitigate unbearable pain.

"I can still remember that warm March day as vividly as yesterday," Mark said. "I was cutting up in a midmorning typing class when the principle, Mr. M., interrupted the class, spoke to the teacher, and fetched me out of class. He wouldn't tell me why. I remember that long, long walk down the empty hall to the office — the ominous sense of what was waiting for me and my two sisters. Someone took us home, where my mother, in near hysteria, said that Daddy had killed himself, that he had shot himself in the mouth.

"That moment is frozen into my mind. Nothing inside of me up to that moment had prepared me for this, and I felt then for the first time that bottomless, suffocating, hysterical sorrow of unknown dimensions that would be with me for a long, long, long time. Moments later, my mother and I discovered the bloody pistol in Dad's briefcase with his letter that someone had thoughtlessly delivered to their bedroom. That image would haunt me for years.

"Our family was immediately caught up in the conspiracy of silence surrounding the suicide, and for me, from age seventeen to twenty-seven, I didn't draw a sober breath. I would drink to the point of passing out—the pain and fear and shame and tension would overtake me, thoughts and images would materialize in my head or dreams, and I agonized with these every minute of every day.

"Stronger and stronger drugs in larger and larger quantities could once in a while ease my insides. I got a clear sense that this relief was worth dying for, and that I would do so, soon. And that fear piled on top of everything else. All this went on for the most part in secret and silence, hidden beneath the more or less 'normal' facade I managed to maintain. But I trusted no one. I felt myself getting very old and tired and hopeless."

Strategies for Combating Depression

Enlist constructive friends. Constructive, positive friends are indispensable when depression clouds your vision and you feel afraid, ashamed, or that you want to hide. It's in your best interest to allow others to help you recapture the joy you've lost, reconnect with authentic faith, and refocus your vision on the fulfillment of your personal sense of calling.

If you listen only to yourself, you may hear an inner monologue that goes on constantly, like background noise, sounding something like this: "You might as well give up. How can you claim to be a Christian, when your life is such a mess?"

Although it is possible to learn how to counteract such negativity with positive self-talk, this problem likely will persist if the only voice responding is your own.

Before there were psychiatrists, there were friends who took long walks together, listening, sharing, and caring. Having at least one intimate friend who knows and loves you is a major component of recovery from depression, for "love is patient, love is kind. It does not envy, it does not boast, it is not proud. It is not rude, it is not self-seeking, it is not easily angered, it keeps no record of wrongs. Love does not delight in evil but rejoices with the truth. It always protects, always trusts, always hopes, always perseveres. Love never fails" (1 Cor. 13:4-8).

Engage in healthful (health-restoring) activities. Regular exercise and a healthy diet will make you feel better physically and, consequently, will also improve your mental outlook. You can really capitalize on the values of walking, for instance, when you combine prayer or hymn singing with it, either alone or with other walkers, as described in the book *Prayer Walk*.[4] Try listening to Bible tapes or tapes of inspirational speakers while walking or running. These activities can accomplish both spiritual and physical goals. Engaging in more strenuous physical exercise such as running can release endorphins, a natural analgesic, in your brain, which can improve your mental outlook.

In my (Dave's) experience, time spent outdoors, especially in the mountains, is healing. God speaks to me through the grandeur of the Rockies, the delicate beauty of tiny wildflowers, the delectability of wild mushrooms sautéed in butter, and the awesome power of an afternoon thunderstorm.

Through more than forty years of hunting, I've probably spent *years* in tree stands, waiting for deer or other game, but mostly enjoying the sun rising and the sun setting, as most of the natural world came alive around me in the morning and then retired with the sun later in the day. For some reason, being eyeball to eyeball with a surprised squirrel or a confused chickadee put my lingering depression into perspective.

I say "lingering" because after nearly twenty years of living with it, my depression has finally departed. Through nearly two decades of depression, about ten medications or combinations of medications kept me sane enough to function. For me, the way out of depression came unexpectedly, through the use of certain nutritional supplements that evidently supply micronutrients my brain needed but my diet lacked, even though I thought my diet was fairly balanced. After a very short time of using these supplements, I realized I didn't need Zoloft any more.

One personal illustration sums it up for me. For years, one of my favorite photos has been "Catch of the Day" by Thomas D. Mangelsen, which shows a grizzly bear standing, mouth open, at the top of a waterfall and a sockeye salmon that has, with one final jump, cleared the falls only to land in the bear's mouth. Until recently, this photo had a lot of philosophical meaning for me. I felt it depicted the futility of even the most enormous effort, if not the futility of life itself. After all, the salmon had worked very hard to conquer the force of the river, only to become the bear's lunch. In other words, I identified with the salmon. Now, having come out of depression, I have a similar poster on the wall, with the initials BTB on it: Be the Bear.

I don't mean to imply that supplements of any kind will help everyone with depression, though some products may make this claim. But as a result of these past few months, I have come to believe that proper nutrition is a far more important component to recovery from depression than is ordinarily thought and that anything you can do to improve in this area will only help you toward recovery.[5]

Let yourself relax. Take time to enjoy activities with friends, take vacations with loved ones, and *regularly* get away from all stress for a period of time. You may not be able to totally eliminate depression's effects—the memories of what has happened may always press you down to some degree—but you can learn to manage it proactively instead of feeling that you are at its mercy. This management of time, energies, and resources may seem difficult, especially if you feel victimized by life in one way or another, but taking time to set goals can give you a new sense of mastery of your situation with all its problems. Two books on this subject that we highly recommend are *Margin* and *The Overload Syndrome*, by Richard A. Swenson, MD.[6]

Retreat centers operated by different Christian groups will allow you to spend a long weekend in the mountains or elsewhere in nature, where you can focus on reflection, scriptural study, prayer, and fellowship. These times can be enormously refreshing. You may think you can't afford the luxury of such a retreat, but the truth may be that you can't afford not to go.

Help others in need. Helping those in need can counteract depression. Encouraging and supporting others who are struggling with life's problems, even if their problems are not similar to yours, can refocus your attention. When we love our fellow human beings as a service to God, joy begins to flow back into our lives.

Judy K., whose father hanged himself when she was four, wrote, "I believe the best way to get through depression is to help others. Doing so helps me too. Writing my book, *Trying to Remember—Forced to Forget (My Father's Suicide)*, was therapy for me, but it has helped others too. My websites, www.suicide survivors.org and www.Xlibris.com/JudyRaphaelKletter.html, help other survivors deal with their grief. Now I'm really happy to participate in this book to help others find their way. This is but another opportunity to share my innermost thoughts, feelings, and coping mechanisms in the hope that they will help somebody else."

You might experience similar healing through helping others, but it need not be through helping survivors of suicide. Volunteering at a children's home, a nursing home, a soup kitchen, or even an animal shelter might have a similar effect for you, though we believe your most satisfying volunteer experiences will involve helping other human beings.

Keep a journal. Many depressed pilgrims have found that keeping a journal helps them see more clearly where they've been, where they are, and where they're headed. This activity can be a source of significant insight into the journey you're on.

Perhaps the most significant impact of a journal over the long term is that when you revisit those difficult times with the journal's help, you can recall how really desperate you were. Without the journal, you might easily forget (or suppress) the intensity of the pain, along with the questions your suffering has raised.

In a sense, journaling helps us know ourselves better, since in those pages we describe what and who we care about, as well as other matters of the heart. We record our hopes, dreams, fears, successes, failures, and questions. A journal's pages may ultimately contain more questions than answers, but the questions themselves imply that we believe there are answers, even if we can't discern them now, because we believe that our personal stories are part of a larger story, which has a beginning and an end, all woven together by a Storyteller who will one day reveal to us how it all makes sense.

Become involved in a support group. Many survivors of suicide have found that support groups have been essential in the process of their healing. Mark, who told the beginning of his story earlier in this chapter, attributes his recovery to his involvement first with Alcoholics Anonymous and then with the local Survivors of Suicide support group.

"I was one real hard-to-help, defiant, angry, know-it-all still on his way down, but then I was led into the fellowship of Alcoholics Anonymous and took my last drink and drug on November 2, 1981. This is a blessing beyond description and has given me a new life and purpose and gratitude sweeter than any words can describe. The promises suggested in the program: that we will know a new freedom and a new happiness, we will neither regret the past nor wish to shut the door on it, we will comprehend the word *serenity* and we will know peace, we will see how our experience can benefit others, that feelings of uselessness and self-pity will disappear, our whole outlook and attitude will change, and we will intuitively know how to handle situations that once baffled us—we will suddenly realize that God is doing for us what we could not do for ourselves. Strong words, but they have come true, and continue to come true, every day in every way in my life. I know I need never be alone again—a key thought, because no survivor of suicide can make it alone.

"Then, seventeen or so years after my dad's death, and having never spoken a word to anyone about all I had felt and continued to feel and think about it, I read a story in the newspaper about the survivors support program. As I read that article, the words used to describe the feelings of survivors just slammed me—talk about the overwhelming sorrow, the shame, the loneliness, and the silence—and I knew the time and place had arrived for me, ready or not. In the group, it was a truly anxious three weeks or so waiting for what I could see was inevitable: I was going to be asked to tell the group something of my story. So I revisited that dark, bottomless abyss of anguish and shared the details for the first time—all the pain and fear and regret and dreams and sorrow and isolation; how much I missed my daddy, his Old Spice smell, the feel of him; how much I needed him; how much I wanted him to be a part of the lives of my children and his grandchildren; how afraid I was without him in the world—all of it. How I had lived in my mind a thousand times his almost incomprehensible final days when he had gathered the implements of his destruction, planned it out, wrote his letter, considered those of us he loved, and anticipated raising the handgun to his mouth. Just the unspeakable terror of all that, which as an unwilling partici-pant, I relived with him over and over again, and the terror of it just would leave me shaken.

"Over the next two or three years, I heard countless simi-lar stories told by people who, when they arrived, all seemed to believe, like I had, that 'this' sorrow was something they could never live through. They were certain they would never laugh again, never feel happy, ever. And listening to them, my dark bottomless pit of pain grew smaller and clearer, and the fear of going in and never returning just went away.

"With absolutely no reservations, today I am a most grate-ful recovering alcoholic and drug addict, a most grateful sur-vivor of my daddy's suicide. I am grateful beyond words to what I know today is a loving God, who has always been with me and has sent me this survivors group and Alcoholics Anony-mous and the healing and joy and assurances I know in the depths of my heart."

Difficult as it may be to start attending a support group, you will be amazed by the degree to which your issues and con-cerns are common to others. As you listen and participate week by week, you may find that these fellow strugglers are the most understanding and supportive group of people you have ever known, and very likely you will come to count them among your best friends.

Beyond that, you'll find a context in which remarkable healing and reversals can take place, as illustrated by Mark's postscript to a recent email: "The other week, I picked up a wind chime from a local metalsmith. It was crafted from the .38-caliber revolver my dad used to take his life. I had found the gun a year after my mother's death. It still, after all these years, had the spent shell casing in it. It took the wind out of me to see it, to think of it. My whole life, I had been haunted by this gun and images and thoughts about it. Now it is no more a gun; rather, like the butterfly, it has been transformed into a thing of beauty.

"Some nights I wake up in the middle of the night and hear the chimes, and it is the most beautiful, delicate, and sublime sound. It gives me such grateful and happy and loving thoughts. My uncle John always felt responsible for my father's death, because he gave Dad the gun. Now I plan to take this chime over to my uncle John's grave and let him know that all is well, that there is peace and acceptance and surrender where there once was only torment."

The Wedge

I don't know you; you don't know me
That's not the way it used to be
Before . . . you know, before . . . he
Left us . . . prematurely.

Initially our hearts were fused
For losing him produced
Pain beyond all mind, confusing
Everything that mattered.

We cared, we shared, defied despair
And tears became your nightly prayer
But words of him I could not bear
So then we wandered on . . . nowhere.

At first the wedge went undiscerned
Survival was our main concern
But separate griefs, so taciturn,
And pride that let no one inside,
And needs that could not be denied
Drove apart the man and bride.

Could anything have intervened
To stop the wedge that came between
Two former friends who might have been
Still one?

Only this, though hard to do
For men, and for some women, too:
Let someone in to share your pain
To walk with you and not refrain
From speaking truth, though this is rare.
Share your grief, and there's a chance
Your pain will wane, your joy enhance.

—DAVID B. BIEBEL[1]

CHAPTER 6

Preserving Relationships
in the Aftermath of Suicide

Here's a little-known and rarely discussed fact about grief: it's a better wedge than it is a glue. If you're early in the process of grieving your loss, you might wonder how this can be true. After all, suicide usually drives survivors together so forcefully that it seems nothing could ever pull them apart—as if the pain should superglue their hearts together. Most survivors do not realize that their relationships (*all* of their relationships) are now at risk.

How your relationships fare long-term will depend on your anticipation and processing of the wide variety of reactions of others and how you interact with them. Unfortunately, some fragmentation of relationships is more or less inevitable, but if you work at it, it is possible to preserve and even improve the relationships most important to you, as is evident from the following true story, adapted from Dave's recently revised and reprinted book *How to Help a Heartbroken Friend.*[2]

One October day in 1989, Jenny's twenty-one-year-old daughter, Angie, was talking with her boyfriend about their future. It wasn't really an argument, but in the middle of it, she got up and walked into another room (with him following), picked up his handgun, swung it around, and it went off. The police recorded Angie's death as an accidental, self-inflicted gunshot wound since there was no depression, no suicidal ideation, no clues. Nobody will ever know if it was intentional or not.

"As you know," Jenny wrote to me, "Christians can be less than kind, and this is a superb gossip opportunity. If one more person says, 'Read your Bible and pray, dear,' I may become unkind myself."

At first, people visited and called, sent cards, and brought food. This was especially helpful, because Jenny's husband and their five other children still needed to eat. It was all Jenny could do to heat up what had been provided and nearly impossible for her to function well enough to carry on her normal routine.

What kept Jenny sane was a professional counselor who allowed her to yell in anger at God about the unfairness of it all. The counselor also taught her enough coping skills to survive the journey, including exercise, relaxation techniques, visualization techniques, blocking, remembering that others also hurt, taking parenting one day at a time, journaling, and personal two- to three-day retreats.

The only coping strategy that connected her directly with another person, however, was to "call someone." In other words, if she wanted help, she had to ask for it—a very difficult thing for a devastated person to do, until the only other option is jumping off a high bridge with a short rope around your neck. Heartbreak is a lonely road.

What made it worse was Jenny's feeling that everybody, including God, had turned their backs on her. "Friends and acquaintances literally walked away," Jenny wrote, "crossed the street, turned around in a store aisle, quickly walked past me, and so on. I expected they would be there for us and allow us to hurt," Jenny added. "I know they do care but simply have no understanding of how to demonstrate that. Love is not enough; it has to be love with action. Love enough to carry a piece of my pain as they share my hurt. The church was our major social life, so our social structure fell apart. We were just plain ignored by most of our church, judged by some. I really struggle with the realization that my non-Christian friends have been there much more than my Christian friends. Why?"

One friend leveled with her: "You guys have been through so much [a whole series of crises], and you always thanked God through it all, smiling along the way. You're crying now, and we don't know what to do with you."

"Well," Jenny noted, "I don't know what to do with me either!"

Her pastor didn't come over until a month after the funeral, and when he did, he said, "I have trouble dealing with death." But the real kicker occurred when a letter arrived from her own brother, a Protestant minister, saying, "I can't absolve her; you'll have to accept that she's probably in hell."

By contrast, a person with no theological ax to grind might hug Jenny and, after using some expletive to describe her trouble, say, "Fate is fate, but friends are friends. If we don't help each other, nobody else will."

Thankfully, Jenny had a casual friend who sent her two to three cards a month that said, "I know you hurt and I care." Another friend would come and take her shopping or out for lunch. But the greatest love she experienced was from her husband, partly as a result of the early intervention of the counselor.

"Our counselor knelt in front of us," Jenny said, "emphasizing that we were different and we would grieve differently and we needed to respect each other's way through this and support each other wherever we were. Our marriage, good before, is stronger now."

Such a wise and compassionate counselor is often the key to the survival of relationships after the suicide of a loved one, because it is almost impossible to objectively perceive the subtle changes in interpersonal dynamics and how to preserve the bonds of caring that still exist.

How the Wedge Works: The Marital Relationship

Take my (Dave's) word for it. Extreme loss of the type we have experienced is one of the Evil One's most effective strategies for tearing asunder what God has joined together. Statistics regarding the percentage of couples who divorce after the death of a child differ, and it's a question well worth further study, but the death of a child puts such stress on a marriage that there's a real risk that divorce will result. I never thought it would happen to me, but it did—more than twenty years after the death of Jonathan. Not much has been written about such delayed fallout, but the main point, as far as I can see, is that the wedge of grief slipped its very thin edge between us early on, and twenty years of life's hammering on it finally split us apart.

People Grieve Differently

Even when two people grieve the same loss, they will not grieve in the same way, with the same intensity, or for the same duration. No two women will grieve identically. No two men will grieve identically. In terms of marriage, men and women generally handle their pain differently.

Women feel freer to cry; men try to be strong (even while crying on the inside). Women want to talk about it; men don't.[3] Women want to get it out and deal with it, often in a group context; men internalize it—deny it, drown it (with alcohol), dull it (with drugs), or try to escape it via any number of inappropriate means. This approach ultimately leads to depression, workaholism (working nonstop in order to avoid feeling one's grief), and a variety of other dysfunctional or self-destructive behaviors, many of which are also destructive to relationships with others, including one's spouse.

The implication of these typical differences between men and women is that misunderstandings are inevitable, not only between any two individuals affected by the same event but especially between men and women affected by the same event, regardless of how long they have known each other or how deeply they love each other.

Ginger wrote, "When we lost our only child, Todd, my husband and I grieved entirely differently, which at times made it very difficult on our marriage. We were okay for about three months, as we both were very stunned and distraught. And Larry experienced recurring nightmares and trauma because he found our son (who had shot himself in the mouth with a shotgun). So we not only looked out for each other at first; we almost walked on eggshells around each other, not wanting to bring anything up about that horrible day. Everyday things that used to bug us (like Larry not picking up after himself or me cracking my knuckles) no longer mattered at all; they just seemed like, and are, stupid, trivial things.

"But at the same time, we did not communicate very much with each other. We talked separately to his sister or to our own psychiatrists, but we didn't share with each other about our feelings. That was a mistake, because at times I became angry, thinking Larry had gotten over our son's death, and he became angry because he felt he hurt more because he found Todd (which is somewhat true—I remembered what Todd looked like, while Larry had that awful image stuck in his mind from when he found him).

"Deep down, I was very angry at Larry because I had wanted to go to the funeral home and just hold Todd's hand and hug him once more before they worked on him, and Larry would not let me. I was in such a stupor that I didn't demand it, but I should have. I remember telling Larry that they could cover Todd's head and it would be okay, but he still insisted, 'No!' Larry was so traumatized that I didn't push it. It's a regret I still carry to this day, though I no longer hold it against Larry. I did not know, until almost a year after Todd's death, that when Larry broke down Todd's bathroom door and discovered him, he threw his truck keys at Todd, and said to him, 'I can't fix this!'

"He had told everyone else but instructed them not to tell me. When he finally told me about it (he felt extremely guilty for throwing his keys at our son's dead body) I was offended that he had not confided in me earlier, though he had told everyone else. I came to think that he must think more of all the others than he thought of me. Now I know that he was trying to protect me from being hurt any further. I too withheld things from him, not wanting to put him through any more.

"Anyway, the bottom line is that we didn't share, didn't talk together, didn't cry together, and that total lack of communication almost destroyed us. We both finally learned through our counseling to let each other grieve in their own way, to give each other space, and to open up to each other when we needed to without being worried we would send the other one into a deeper depression if we communicated how we were feeling that day."

Staying Connected

With courage and persistence, couples can manage their differences in grieving. But first these differences must be acknowledged, even embraced (for in the long term, such God-given differences can be an asset to a couple rather than a liability). Here are a few more comments from your fellow pilgrims.

"Our marriage has definitely been affected! *All* communication is difficult since Wayne's death," Ann wrote. "Wayne's stepfather is trying to protect me and not bring me more pain; therefore, he withdraws and hides his pain and grief, even when I ask and explain that I'm worried about him too.

"I read Iris Bolton's *My Son, My Son* within the first month, and I'm glad I did! The book made me understand how we need to make the effort and commitment to be a family unit and work together to get through this. We've talked about it some and we both understand it, but there are days when it's almost impossible or we just don't have the extra energy.

"I recently started emailing my husband. I send notes that simply say 'I love you' or I share my poetry with him. I figure I can reassure him that I love him, plus it's a safer way to communicate sometimes about things like my poetry about Wayne."

FINDING YOUR WAY

Preserving Your Marriage

Talk about your fears, anger, and other emotions without condemning yourselves or each other. You may find it less threatening to do this by discussing examples of suicide from books, magazines, movies, or the news with a focus on how the people involved were affected.

Link with a support system such as a support group, a professional counselor, or an objective friend who will help you to express your thoughts and feelings to each other. The most common issue that divides couples is not grief or depression but the lack of ability to communicate their way through conflict. Although communication of any depth is affected by grief or depression, a skilled counselor can help you move through conflict toward greater understanding and a deeper relationship.

Despite your pain, celebrate your individuality and differences. Allow your spouse to feel what she feels, to say what

Marlene wrote, "I lost my twenty-four-year-old son to suicide in 1997. My marriage to my son's father had ended twelve years prior. When my son died, I had been married only six years to my current husband, who has been extremely supportive of me. It was an awful time for me. During the first year after my son's death, I truly lived in a vacuum, or at least I felt that way. It was a very surreal time for me, for all of us really. *Emotionally, I was numb. I didn't want to be touched sexually. My husband and I had previously enjoyed a very good sexual relationship, which gave us great joy. How could I allow myself to experience joy? It was inconceivable. I remember it took months before our first failed attempt. Failed because I responded and then felt guilty for responding.*[4]

"Therapy was a huge help for us. I am very blessed in that I have a wonderful, compassionate, caring husband who didn't give up on me."

he needs to say, to weep or not to weep, or even to remain silent. One of the most valuable gifts you can give each other during this time is to accept each other *without judgment or trying to fix* the personal pain of your spouse.

Remember the qualities that attracted you to each other. Emphasize the strengths and downplay the weaknesses. Remember that section from Revelation 2, where John is instructed to chastise the church at Ephesus for having left its first love? Part of the Lord's remedy is to "repent and do the deeds you did at first" (Rev. 2:5 NASB). Once upon a time, before your tragedy changed everything, you were in love—hearts, hopes, and bodies intertwined in living with and for each other. You could try to recapture even a small part of that by doing what you did at first and seeing what it rekindles. Start small—with a flower, a gift, a card, a movie, dinner at your favorite restaurant. You might use the exercise in appendix 2, "Starting Over: Weaving New Dreams Together," as a starting point in reviving your sense of shared life, including your goals, hopes, and dreams. It could help you focus on what could be instead of what was or might have been.

Judy T. wrote that after the suicide of her daughter Lea, their other daughter, Betsy, dropped out of college and moved home. "She, Paul, and I were very much a three-legged stool. Paul wanted to go to groups and classes to learn 'how to do grief.' I dropped out of my second year on my master's in counseling and taught four-year-olds in a university day-care center for one semester. I worked from 7:00 a.m. until 12:30 p.m. and came home and slept all afternoon and cried all night. The hugs and nurturing needs of the children were the 'group work' I needed.

"Paul is a minister. Two weeks after Lea's death, he went back to work, and a small powerful group decided that he needed to be 'over it.' They perceived the fact that he wasn't over it yet as an unforgivable weakness on his part and proof that he wasn't fit to be clergy! He had to fight for his vocation and livelihood.

That fight took all his energy. It took two years, but he won. Two years later, when we were ready, he received a call to another church—where we are happy to be.

"The conflict at the church made our different grieving styles very difficult and conflicted. Neither of us felt the other was doing what needed to be done. We couldn't talk because it hurt me too much to hear about the players in the church conflict, which was all that he wanted to talk about. It hurt him too much to talk about our loss because I had the time to try to cope with that and he couldn't go there. At one point, the bishop offered him a 'mental health leave.' Paul felt too stigmatized by that and didn't even tell me about it until it was too late. Had it been offered as a 'bereavement leave' I think he might have been able to accept it.

"I decided to continue my master's at a different school, which was the perfect opportunity for me to make my own set of friends and to join a new support group that had nothing to do with the community that was trying to destroy my husband. If I hadn't been able to get away and start new on my own life, I doubt our marriage would have survived."

Preserving Your Family Relationships

The wedge affects the relationships of all the survivors in the deceased's network of relationships. This is particularly true in the family network. Let's say that before the death, there were five people in a particular family network: two parents, two boys, and one girl. The youngest son took his own life. Before that point, the family could be described as: A + B + C + D + E = their system of relationships. The father and mother are A and B respectively. The older son is C. The daughter is D. The youngest son is E.

Each knew and related to the others in certain ways. A knew B as the mother of C, D, and E. He also knew her as his wife. B knew A in a similar way. But there were other, more subtle aspects in the relationships of A and B (as well as C and D) because of E. For example, imagine that E had a sense of humor that calmed the waters when conflict arose. When Mom and Dad would make much ado about nothing, E would make them laugh, and they'd realize they didn't need to sweat the small stuff. With the comedian gone, the small stuff will likely escalate in its apparent importance the next time there is conflict.

The survivors have not only lost a family member to suicide; they have also lost the part of each other that was known to them in some way through the influence or presence of the deceased. Let's say that in this family's case, the comedian (E) would often pull practical jokes on his siblings (C and D), sometimes on both of them at once. The siblings would always get mad, rant and rave for a while, and sometimes even scuffle with each other, saying things they really didn't mean—much to the amusement of E, who would eventually crack a joke, and they would all laugh it off. As they grew up together, C and D learned things about themselves and about each other as a result of E's shenanigans.

After one person is removed from the family system through suicide, it seems to each survivor that all the others have changed. Thus, the family is not as "familiar" as before. But what has really happened is that the family system of relationships has changed, especially the way in which each survivor knows the others. When this anxiety is added to the emotional chaos in each person's heart to the point that one or more parties blame the other(s) for whatever seems wrong, the wedge of grief is doing its work.

FINDING YOUR WAY

Keeping the Family Together

Commit yourselves to truthful communication. Find ways to express to each other your deepest feelings and needs. Some people can verbalize their grief on paper (in a personal journal, poetry, or a book) but avoid actually discussing their feelings with another person or group. This is one place where I (Dave) wish I had it all to do over, for although I could write my deepest feelings on paper, to express them to another person, which made me far more vulnerable, was nearly impossible. So in a sense, even though my books have helped many others find their way along the path of grief, and writing them helped me to some degree, my avoidance of the more threatening disclosures that might have arisen in one-on-one communication within the family setting was one way the wedge got its point between us.

Don't misunderstand me—journaling is a good idea; poetry gushes from the heart; books are sometimes driven from the energy of grief. But in the end, these are of far less value than preserved and enhanced relationships. Things that preserve and enhance relationships include heart-to-heart talks; tears; acceptance and affirmation; freedom for expressions of anger, frustration, guilt, and regrets; plus a generous helping of forgiveness and grace.

Cherish the silence when that's all there is. When there's nothing to be said, nothing *must* be said. (You know this well from your experiences with others during the period surrounding the funeral, when a lot of people with nothing substantial to say were not wise enough to just be there silently.) In your family setting, no one should be forced to "share." During such times, embracing, holding hands, or even a gentle touch on the shoulder says, without words: "We're in this together. This is our problem, and we'll find our way through it together, as long as it takes and no matter how hard the way becomes, until we know that we are on the other side of this wilderness into which we have been thrust against our wills."

If there was a suicide note that tried to blame another family member or the entire family, forgiveness and affirmation are needed by all who were indicted. This type of note can run the gamut from "I just couldn't live with her nagging anymore" to "I told you that kid would be the death of me," or "I know you've all been waiting for me to get out of the way so you could have my money and all my things. So I hope you're all happy now."

Regardless of how irrational such charges may be, they still hurt in ways that defy logic, which is why the accused will also need to forgive the deceased, whether or not the note has any factual basis. Otherwise, the survivor(s) may become captive to the last words of someone they can no longer confront with the truth.

One way to resolve issues related to a note like this is to burn it privately, and possibly to bury the ashes as a way of returning the communication to its author. Or the ashes might be thrown to the wind, as a symbol of God's Spirit, who is the only one truly capable of rescuing meaning and resurrecting relationships from the fire you've all been through. Perhaps your pastor or other spiritual advisor would be willing to help with such a ceremony. The main thing isn't what is done, how it's done, or by whom but that you all agree on what it means and that you commit yourselves to never deviate from that agreement, publicly or privately.

For many survivors, it seems that life has ended, dreams have died, and meaning has flown as a result of the suicide of their loved one. Common as these feelings may be, it is possible to start over, with whoever is left in the family circle, and weave new dreams. As you dream together and help each other fulfill those dreams, your relationships will be enhanced because you'll be focused on what could be, not what was or what might have been. Use the exercise in appendix 2 to help you envision your future together.

No Going Back

... after suicide there is no going back
no gently returning to that good peace of mind
wherein God's in our universe and all's well with the world
because we are whole no more, rather shattered and

struggling to withstand the shards of horror that shine
reflected in the eyes of our acquaintances as they check our
crown for thorns and our expressions for evidence of collusion.
Was it a phone call we failed to return, a favor, a smile?

... after suicide there is no going back
no gently returning to that good hope we love in one another
when earth tugs only at our feet, not at our lungs, and leaves our
hearts at liberty to risk, to dare, to trust, and to tame.

In retrospect, there is no going back, no explanation, no
reason good enough to justify our lack of interest in one
whose loneliness could only be assuaged by death.
... after suicide there is no going back, only memories.

—LUCY[1]

CHAPTER 7

Suicide Survival in Special Situations

Surviving the Suicide of Your Spouse

You have lost your partner, love, helpmate, and co-parent of your children. Now you have to make decisions or manage things alone that in the past, you and your spouse managed together or your spouse took care of. Just writing checks and paying bills can be a daunting task if you have not previously had the responsibility of doing this. Sometimes your pile of bills, notices, and other correspondence requiring attention will seem overwhelming. You will likely feel abandoned, angry, and the whole gamut of emotions that accompany deep grief. Your first year on this journey will be similar to that of other survivors, especially the feeling that part of you has been amputated. If mere survival weren't difficult enough, you may feel some responsibility for what happened, or others may imply this in one way or another.

To further complicate matters, early in your survival you may consider filling the hole in your life with another person. While another relationship may feel good to you in certain ways, it will likely not be good for you and your new friend until you have resolved issues related to your deceased spouse. Otherwise, you cannot really be free enough to develop a healthy, mutually beneficial relationship without loading your new companion with baggage he or she should not feel obligated to carry.

Consider this letter we received while we were writing this chapter:

Hello David,

I found your email address while researching "suicide" on the Internet. The title of the book that you are currently writing caught my attention. . . . This is my situation: I am in love with, and engaged to, a woman who lost a man she loved to suicide eleven years ago. There is a thirteen-year-old son from this relationship. My fiancée mentions her former husband's name, or the suicide, or what he did or said, every day. When I try to express my feelings or thoughts about my job, my family, or my friends, she relates every situation to the suicide. This makes me uncomfortable. I imagine the guilt of losing someone to suicide would be everlasting, but it is difficult to live with someone who feels like she has to atone for that loss for the rest of her life.

Sometimes I think that if I was brought into her life to help her heal, then so be it. I will work as the Lord wants me to. As much as I want to find true love and happiness, I can't change what is already written for me.

We have spent many nights talking about what happened—her telling me about him (things which as another man, I didn't want to know). I listened still. She has a bookcase full of books and tapes on suicide. After his death, she attended many gatherings and support groups. She got help and surrounded herself with people that had been through a similar experience . . . and one might think these things would have helped her resolve some of it.

She claims to have found love again with me. But it seems that everything she does is because of her regret and loss, and not because she is truly in love with me. So I feel cheated because I am in love with a person who will forever feel guilty for not being able to help her first love out of suicide.

If there is anything you can do to help me be happy, and understand or help this woman, please let me know.

Sincerely,
W.

Dave responded:

Dear W.,

I recognize this pattern a bit from my own journey with losses in that I have lived with the grief, guilt, and all that goes with it for more than twenty-five years now. For most of that time, I thought or spoke of Jonathan nearly every day. Though I didn't realize it then, this implied to my other children that he (or his memory) was more valuable to me than they were, which wasn't true as far as I was concerned, but it felt true to them, and that is what mattered.

Most likely, your friend is not aware of the level of her continuing attachment to her former spouse, nor how this attachment is affecting everyone in her current system of relationships. The fact that she probably could not have prevented what happened may not change the way she relates to it, at least for now, for this is not a matter of the mind but of the heart, which needs healing. She does not need to forget him in order to love you or others, but she needs to know that with her heart *and* mind. One good thing is that the level of her pain is an indicator of her potential for joy, if she can resolve to move ahead.

As for you and your happiness . . . this is a very hard question, as I don't know you very well. But I would say if you feel that it is your calling to comfort or rescue her, this may also interfere with the kind of mutually edifying love that marriage can be.

Sincerely,
Dave Biebel

FINDING YOUR WAY

As a Surviving Spouse

Avoid making major decisions without obtaining objective advice. You may wonder how you will manage financially, especially if there is little or no insurance or you don't have savings or investments. Some people in your situation liquidate their assets and move to another location as soon as possible, partly to reduce their anxiety and partly to escape the memories associated with their prior home, community, or church. Quick decisions made with many things weighing on your mind will likely result in the unnecessary loss of resources, from possessions to people who might have been able to support or help you.

Even if you have lost a major portion of your income and financial security as a result of this tragedy, you probably have some assets that need proper management. A thorough review of your entire situation with a trustworthy professional will prove invaluable over time. Even better, solicit and compare several opinions, then implement the best strategies.

If you have children, allow others to help you care for them. This will be difficult, because fear of losing them too will likely haunt you for some time. When you have a lot on your mind, it's easy to become distracted while driving, so it's wise to let others take over your responsibilities in the carpool for a month or two and transport your children to appointments or other activities.

Resist the temptation to use drugs or alcohol or other destructive activities to cope with the pain. Some survivors turn to drinking, taking illegal or prescription drugs, overspending, overeating, partying, sexual experiences, gambling, or other destructive behaviors. None of these really help heal the pain. All are destructive and can become addictions over time.

Avoid the rebound effect. You will feel extremely alone and lonely after the death of your spouse. But take enough time to work through your grief. A rebound relationship may cause you more grief than happiness in the long run. Neither grieving nor loving come with timetables. But with all the issues you're facing, it seems prudent to put off the serious pursuit of romance for at least a year and to use that time to let the Lord mend your broken heart.

Surviving Suicide as a Single Parent

The loneliness and grief following my daughter's suicide were barely manageable for me (Sue) as a single parent. I had no spouse with whom to share my sorrow. I could see the difficulties my son was having because of his sister's death, but I felt helpless to help him.

Half of my purpose and meaning in life was gone. My son lived with his father for half of the year, and I simply didn't know what to do with myself when he was gone. The need to have someone to take care of, besides myself, was intense and so very painful. I remember walking into a grocery store where

As a Surviving Single Parent

Let others help you. Support of family and friends is vital. Let them clean, do laundry, and pick up groceries for you. Ask them to help with your other children (if you have any). Some friends will be good listeners—something you really need. They will let you say the same things over and over until you don't need to say them again.

Avoid isolation. It is easy to hide when you're a single parent. Reach out to others, even though this is difficult when you are in so much pain. A support group, such as Survivors of Suicide, and a counselor can be your survival lifeline.

Avoid easing the pain with things like food, work, drugs and alcohol, illicit sexual experiences, or even just staying in bed. These ultimately prolong the grief process. I (Sue) was often so depressed that I went to bed Friday night after work and got up only to eat and let the dog out until Monday morning, when I got out of bed to return to work. This went on for several months. No one knew. Instead of helping, this pattern only deepened my depression and grief.

I had shopped for years and having a panic attack before I had even gone ten feet inside the door. The shelves of food shouted, "You have no reason to come here now." I left and didn't return to that store for several months.

Surviving Suicide as a Stepparent

After the loss of a stepchild to suicide, stepparents often feel like outsiders. They don't know what is expected of them or how best to help their spouse or the sibling(s) of the deceased deal with the child's death. Communication with the biological parent may be difficult if the marriage is relatively recent. If there were relational problems with the deceased, and even if not, the stepparent may feel some guilt or remorse.

Jerry wrote that he wondered, *If I had not married Linda, would her son [Paul] still be alive?* Jerry said that his five-year marriage to Linda was strained for a long time after Paul's death. "I was able to help Linda grieve with quiet feelings and an 'in the background' position," he said. "As time passed, she became more aware of others in the same place, other survivors, and I encouraged her to become involved. As she did, she began to heal. As she healed, she was able to help others deal with their own losses."

Sometimes the primary role of the stepparent is to try to be strong and hold things together while their partner grieves the loss of the child, although this apparent lack of grief can be misunderstood. Jan said that after his stepson Wayne took his life, "I have had to suppress my own feelings so that I can be there for Ann. She has said that she cannot be there for me, and I understand that. However, she gets upset that I'm not grieving the way she is. It is also hard to deal with her fragile feelings. This has made things very difficult in our marriage."

If you're in this situation, it is important to be there for your spouse, to listen, and to offer support where needed. But don't expect to be able to fix things. As Jerry said, "This is one of those times that you cannot 'touch the hurt and make it all better.'"

FINDING YOUR WAY

As a Surviving Stepparent

Find someone who can support you. Feeling like you must carry the load for a long time can lead to resentment, which is deadly to a relationship. You need a friend (of the same gender)[2] who will let you vent your frustrations and fears without loading you with advice. Family counseling and/or support groups can be helpful, especially if you and your spouse will attend together.

Remember that your spouse's grief is very personal and at times overwhelming. You can't expect to understand the depth of those feelings unless your spouse will let you inside the pain. Don't try to force this issue, as this may create resistance and resentment. If your spouse's grief is negatively affecting your sexual relationship, this is another area where forcing the issue will just create more problems than it solves. In this situation, women prefer to be held and nurtured. Men prefer to be able to release the tension through mutually enjoyable sex.[3]

Guard against feeling left out. Contribute where you can. Offer to do the cooking, cleaning, laundry, banking, bill paying, carpooling, shopping, or anything your spouse usually handles. Your spouse will appreciate that you were thoughtful enough to take on some of the burdens.

Surviving Suicide as a Grandparent

Grandparents are often overlooked in the aftermath of a child's suicide. This is not intentional, but most of the attention and support is focused on the parents and siblings. Grandparents aren't often consulted about such things as funeral and burial arrangements, and they very often have opinions and wishes in this area. Grandparents can offer wisdom and comfort based on life experience.

Judy T.'s parents experienced a double grief when their granddaughter Lea took her own life; they grieved over their loss of Lea, plus they grieved for Judy's loss of Lea.

I (Sue) asked my mother to describe how Shannon's death affected her. Mom wrote: "Shannon was our first grandbaby, and I adored her. She was with us when she sat up in her crib for the first time. She was with us when she took her first steps by herself. I took her to church one Sunday when a dedication service was being held, and I went up front with her and dedicated her to the Lord. Shannon was the joy of my life, and I loved her so very much.

"The day Shannon died, I felt like someone had stabbed me in the heart. I wanted to go to my bedroom and cry and wail and scream, but the neighbors came to say how sorry they were to hear about Shannon. I knew they meant well, and I appreciated their caring, but I felt like my guts were being pulled out of my body. I couldn't break down and go to pieces because I had to be strong for the rest of the family.

"I don't remember ever blaming or being mad at God. I just didn't understand why Shannon would do something like that. She must have been so unhappy. Did she do this for attention? Didn't she know that she was taking too many pills, or was this an accident and she really didn't mean to die? Why, why, why?

"The day Shannon was buried was horrible to get through. We were at Sue's all day and at her church for so many hours, all afternoon and evening. Thank the Lord for the good friends who came and stayed with us and helped us get through the day and evening.

"I read in *Our Daily Bread* in August 2003: 'I have been through the valley of weeping, the valley of sorrow and pain. But the God of all comfort was with me, at hand to uphold and sustain.' That's the way I feel now, that I have been through the valley of sorrow and pain. But, thank God, he's brought me through that valley. He didn't leave me there.'"

As a Surviving Grandparent

Acknowledge your sense of loss. You have lost someone you love deeply. You too have lost your future with this child. Additionally, you grieve deeply because of what your own child is going through. Talk about these things with someone who will listen without having to tell you all the sorrows they have known.

Offer to help where you can. Many important decisions must be made in the wake of a suicide, including arrangements for the funeral and the disposition of the body. Take care to respect your own child's preferences here, but let them know you are available for advice if needed. If you are financially better off than your child, you might offer to help with expenses related to the funeral, including travel expenses for other family members who may wish to attend. Other ways you might help include caring for the home and other practical details such as food preparation or taking the surviving children to your home, if this is practical.

Find a support group. Some communities have support groups for grandparents who are survivors. If yours does not, you could inquire about how to start one. See the resources section for a list of organizations that are ready, able, and eager to help with this.

When Survivors Are Children

One day when she was four years old, Judy K. found her father's body hanging from a rope in the bathroom. Because of the way her mother and family handled the suicide, it took Judy *fifty years* to discover and deal with the truth. She has told her story in the book *Trying to Remember, Forced to Forget (My Father's Suicide)*.[4] "My mother denied that my father's death was suicide and never talked about it," Judy wrote to us. "According to her, he had a heart attack and died in the hospital (even though I was the one who had found him). Nobody talked to me about the suicide. I was so disturbed and confused about what I saw that I was committed to a mental institution for three years.

"I have no doubt that my mother, for whatever reasons I will never know (denial, shame, protection of me and/or herself), thought she was shielding me from something that would hurt me more if I knew the truth. I lived behind this wall from 1948 to 1998 until after my mother's death, when I felt free to rediscover my past. The very important message I would like to emphasize is: never shield young children from the truth. If you do, you are causing them more harm than good. Young children do know what is going on and should be included in the grieving process."

Young children (up to age eight) often think of death as temporary and reversible. They expect to see again the person who has died, as if she is on a trip somewhere and will return soon.

They also tend to think concretely. For example, after Jonathan died at age three, I (Dave) was told that some of his little friends had packed toys into their wagons in preparation for going to see him in heaven, where they'd been told he had gone.

If your child considers death a scary thing, you may find him hiding from it in a closet, under the bed, or in one of his secret places, such as a tree house or even inside a hollowed-out tree trunk in the back woods.

Young children usually engage in magical thinking. Debbie told us that her six-year-old daughter thought her deceased brother, Josh, was mad at her. "I've been writing letters to him in heaven, and he hasn't answered me," Brittany said.

Young children also tend to be very literal. They may believe that their anger has killed their loved one. This, of course, can produce a lifelong struggle with misplaced and debilitating guilt if it is not resolved, usually with the help of a trained professional.

Young children lack verbal skills and often are not able to describe their feelings. As a result, they may act out their feelings. For example, instead of saying, "I am extremely frustrated and disappointed that Daddy left without even saying goodbye," they might pick a fight with the neighbor kid over something insignificant.

Older children (ages nine to twelve) have a more realistic view of death and know that it can't be reversed. They are less literal and magical in their thinking. Their view of death and suicide may have been influenced by heavy-metal music, though this is more likely during the teen years.

They may seem temporarily out of control or driven to do things that are out of character with who they really are, such as tormenting a family pet, breaking things unnecessarily, or getting into trouble at school. This type of acting out is a normal reaction to trauma for children. Some adults overreact to the misbehavior of their formerly "good" children in ways that create more trauma and anxiety, which can cause significant harm to the child's psyche and the parent-child relationship in general.

Adolescent survivors also need help in understanding and expressing their grief. Although teens usually seek support from their peers, many adolescents report that this sharing is hindered after a suicide because now they feel different from their peers and it is difficult for them to share with others how their loved one died.

A surviving parent may try to counsel their adolescent through this time, but it is nearly impossible for most grieving adults to separate themselves enough from their own grief to understand and support an adolescent. Most likely, the help of qualified third parties such as school counselors, pastors, physicians, and others will be more effective.

If adolescents do not receive the help they need (either because it's not available or through avoidance), they may deny or bury their grief, which may later surface in the use of drugs and alcohol, social problems, declining school performance, low self-esteem, and depression.

Depression in Surviving Children

Children of any age can become depressed, and this is a natural reaction following the suicide of a loved one. Depressed children often have feelings of hopelessness and helplessness. They may feel guilty or worthless. They may say they wish they'd never been born. Other signs of depression in children include:

- Lack of energy—a red flag in normally high-energy children
- Lingering sadness in a normally cheerful child
- Loss of interest in things that used to bring pleasure
- Withdrawal in a previously outgoing child
- Expressions of irritability, anger, or anxiety
- Inability to concentrate
- Changes in eating patterns, leading to weight gain or loss
- Changes in sleep patterns, both insomnia and oversleeping
- New physical complaints, unaccounted-for aches and pains
- Preoccupation with death

These symptoms are similar to the symptoms of depression in adults. If several symptoms persist for more than two weeks,[5] it is time to see a pediatrician, family physician, or child psychiatrist.[6]

FINDING YOUR WAY

When Survivors Are Children

Communicate the truth in love, on their individual level.
For young children, adult explanations such as "Mommy's body is in that box, but her soul is with God" may not connect well with their real questions or issues, which might be: "Did Mommy go away because she was mad at me for being bad the other day? Where did she go? When is she coming back?"

You might respond with something like this: "Mommy can't come home again, dear. Remember how our doggie Rusty got sick and died last year? After we buried him, we didn't have him to play with any more. We were so sad for a long time, but after a while, we were happy and sad at the same time when we remembered him.

"Well, Mommy was sick too. None of us knew how sick she was until it was too late, and we couldn't keep her from hurting herself. She died, and we can't bring her back. So now we will be sad again for a while and we'll miss her a lot, but later when we think of her, we'll be sad and happy at the same time."

With older children, you should discuss suicide as openly as they can handle, depending on their maturity. You should also discuss what they should tell their friends, many of whom will already know that the death was a suicide.

Let your older children know that the person had an illness (depression) that caused her to not be able to see things clearly ("irrational" or "mentally ill" may not communicate what you need to say), including the fact that she was loved and needed by you and them.

Tell them that it's normal to feel a wide range of emotions, from frustration to fear to guilt, and that when they wish to talk about these things, you'll be there to listen. Let them know it's okay if they would rather talk with someone else, because sometimes it's hard to "let it all hang out" with a parent. Have a counselor or counselors lined up in case a child says he needs to talk with somebody.

Do not assume that your children will bounce back quickly from losses as devastating as suicide. Most likely, they will not be able to recover well without your assistance and that of other caring adults who can help them resolve their grief in healthy ways.

Notify the school that you want to know right away if any changes or problems in your children's behavior occur. Also watch for any changes that indicate depression, and be prepared to take the child to see a physician if these symptoms occur.

Dear DJ,

Hey, bud. I just wanted to take a minute to tell you that I love you and I miss you so much. Life just hasn't been the same without you. There is a hole in my life that can never be filled. But I try every day to make things normal again. I know that you would want it that way.

DJ, I wish that you were here. I don't understand why you chose to leave us. I honestly want to believe that you didn't mean to, that you would never choose to leave behind the people who loved you more than life. Yet I know that you made that choice. And honestly, I am not mad. I am just so heartbroken that I cannot even breathe sometimes.

I can't see tomorrow without you because I am blinded by my tears. I know in my heart that you are still here, that your spirit surrounds me, but not hearing your voice or seeing your smile—it's almost unbearable.

I try to remember the good times. I wear your shirt to feel you next to me. You are the first thing on my mind when I wake up, and the last thing on my mind when I go to sleep. You are always in my heart, DJ.

I love you, bud. I miss you terribly. Always.

Until we meet again.

Love, your big sis,
Monica[1]

CHAPTER 8

After the Suicide
of Your Brother or Sister

When you lose a brother or sister to suicide, you lose a relationship that has a bond like no other, a bond that cannot be replaced. Siblings often take this bond for granted and really don't understand its uniqueness until it is broken. One survivor told us that it feels like "part of me has been amputated."

You may feel that you have lost your closest confidant and ally, perhaps your best friend. You have memories of the past with that brother or sister, but the present is irrevocably changed, and the future with your loved one is lost forever. As Monica said, "My baby brother is not ever coming back."

One Brother's Account

This is how Sue's son, Steve, described the details and effect of the death of his sister, Shannon: "Alone. She was gone, and I was alone. Someone who understood me and looked out for me and then she was gone. It was a cold morning, and I was staying home from school so I could be with my friends. Being the last day before Christmas break, it didn't seem to matter much. My freshman year of high school wasn't all that important to me. Looking back, I wonder what would have happened if I had gone to school that morning. She would still be gone, but the image in my head that I have had to live with for twelve years would not be there.

"Five days before Christmas 1991, I found my sister dead in her bed. I remember that day as if it were this morning. It is almost a repeated dream for me, a dream I never seem to wake up from. I was awakened that morning by the screaming of my sister's name. My mom had opened her bedroom door to see if she was okay. She should have been awake by now. I was sleeping downstairs on the couch by the Christmas tree, and when I heard that scream, I jumped up and started running up the stairs. I remember vividly the picture I had in my head as I ran toward my mom. It was a picture of my sister hanging by a rope in her bedroom.

"My sister did not hang herself, but I knew she was dead. I reached her door to find my mom crying. When I walked in, I found Shannon in her bed; her lips were puckered almost like a smile, and her face was a light blue. On the nightstand next to her were my mom's pain medications from her dentist. My mom ran to the phone to call 911, and I just stood there staring at Shannon, knowing that I would never talk to her again, never laugh with her, never see her smile again. She had an amazing smile.

"Somehow the phone ended up in my hand. I don't recall how that came about, but I knew my mom could not speak. The emergency operator was a woman who was very nice and calming, and she instructed me to find out if there was anything I could do to save her. She told me to feel her body to see if there was warmth. I reached down and touched her side. It was warm. She then told me to try and bring her down to the floor so I could start CPR until the paramedics arrived. I grabbed her arm to move her and when I tried to move her to the floor, I found that she was as stiff as a board.

"I was fifteen and I had to feel my sister's stiff body. I have never been able to wash that feeling from my hands. I told the operator she was stiff, and that's when I noticed her electric blanket was on and that's why she was warm. I asked the operator, 'She's dead, isn't she?' The operator paused, 'Yes, son, I'm afraid she is.' I remember how hard my mom was crying, completely uncontrollable tears. Her daughter was gone, her firstborn.

"I ran down the way to my best friend's house. I thought his mom might be home and that she could comfort my mom at this time. I pounded on their door and my friend answered. 'Where is your mom?' I shouted. He replied, 'She's at the store. Why? What's going on?' I told him that Shannon was dead. Dead at age nineteen. She had her whole life ahead of her, and she was gone. Just then his mom came home, and when I told her what was wrong, she followed me to my house. Right at that time the police came. I remember the look on the officer's face because he looked concerned. Not someone there just doing his job, but someone who was concerned. That really struck me.

"By this time, chaos set in. I don't actually remember much of what happened in the minutes that led up to my father showing up. He was called while at work. He didn't know any of the details but had been told to come quickly because Shannon was dead and I wasn't crying. And I wasn't. I think I was in complete and utter shock. The morning was too dramatic for me to shed a single tear if that makes any sense. My dad wanted to see her body, to say goodbye I guess. The coroner came and left, and the paramedics took her body. Friends came over to console us, but I wanted to be alone. It had started to rain, and I went outside and walked. I walked for hours on the empty streets in the pouring rain, soaked and chilled to the bone. I didn't know what else to do, so I walked thinking about her. My sister, my blood, my friend. The day was never ending, and the rain never stopped. When I finally went home, my mom was too upset to notice that I was drenched. I went upstairs and changed and remained silent. I remember my mom and her friends praying, trying to make sense of this whole mess. I also remember thinking that God can't control this one. Shannon chose this fate. She chose to quit.

"In the weeks that followed, everyone tried to come up with a reason she did this, what could have pushed her to do this. The word *accident* came up. I knew then and still know that it was not an accident. They thought she was just trying to get attention, that she really didn't mean to do it. But I know she did. Then my mom and dad started to blame themselves, thinking that if they had only loved her more or talked to her more, this wouldn't have happened. That was not true either. It was no one's fault. Suicide is never anyone's fault. There is nothing they could have done better to make the situation any different. Trying to figure out the reason will drive you mad. There are some other reasons people gave for why she did what she did, but I know for a fact they aren't the reasons. The truth of the matter is that in the last year leading up to her death, she had confided in me more than she ever had before. A year or so prior to her death, we had lost a stepsister to a brain tumor. After that, we had become the closest we had ever been. She told me some things my parents will never know about. Some good, some not so good.

"A few months had passed when a man from my church called me and wanted to hang out with me for the day. He took me to a friend's house, where we took their horses out. We walked a trail that led to a huge open field next to my high school. I walked the horse down to one end of the field, turned him in the direction of the other end, and kicked that horse as hard as I could. He shot out at a full sprint and, for the first time in months, I smiled. The wind forcing back my hair, tears streaming down my face, I let go. For a few moments in time, I let go of the cares and worries of the world. In the twenty seconds or so that it took that horse to reach the end of the field, I felt more alive than I ever had. In fact, I don't remember a time I felt so alive. That is what my sister had lost. She got so bogged down with the emptiness that this life sometimes brings that she forgot how to live. She forgot what hope is.

"To this day, when memories of my sister and the loss I have had to deal with come streaming into my head, when this life just seems unbearable, two words ring out and remind me to push forward and not give up: *I hope.*"

Your Place in the Family System Has Changed

Not only is your relationship with your sibling lost, but your special place and identity in the family system of relationships has also been changed. For example, if you were the youngest child, you may now have to bear the responsibilities of being the oldest or only child. After Shannon died, Steve became the only surviving grandchild on both sides of the family. He felt the burden of responsibilities and obligations that had been his sister's. He felt he had to grow up quickly and assume a role he didn't ask for and wasn't entirely sure he wanted.

Adult children usually expect to share the responsibility of caring for their parents as they grow older. When a sibling is removed from the family circle through suicide, the base of responsibility grows smaller, which can result in resentment toward the deceased. Colleen recalled how angry she was when her forty-two-year-old brother shot himself because this left her alone to deal with all of the family business. Although she understood why he took his life (he had terminal cancer), she was still angry with him.

Linda's daughter shared similar sentiments after the suicide of her brother, Paul. She was angry with him for leaving her to bear alone the responsibility for their parents and grandparents, which they would have shared had Paul survived.

Debbie (the mother of Josh, who took his own life at age fifteen) told us: "My surviving son, Jake, will turn sixteen soon. Seven years ago, he went from being the middle child to being the oldest. Now he is dealing with issues and having life experiences that are new to him and to us. I am sure that many times he has wished his older brother were still here to do things with him that are now up to Mom and Dad, such as teaching him to drive and discussing girls and dating. One of Jake's best friends has an older brother. They fight a lot, like many siblings, and this bothers Jake — I can see it in his eyes — because he would give anything to still have a brother, not to fight with but to be friends with."

Surviving Siblings Often Feel Left Behind and Left Out

Several survivors said that they felt "left behind" in the aftermath of the suicide of their brother or sister. The focus of attention after the horribleness and chaos of a suicide tends to be on the parents of the deceased. Parents can become so immersed in their own intense pain and loss that they forget that the surviving siblings still need their parents' attention and support.

Surviving siblings may be left to fend for themselves. A child may be told, "You be sure to take care of your parents" and wonder, *Who will take care of me?*

Even older siblings can struggle deeply after the death of a brother or sister. Without the support of their family, some may fall into a very deep pit before they find a way to climb out. Marlene's daughter, Kerry, was twenty-five at the time of her younger brother's suicide. "My daughter was extremely close to her brother," Marlene wrote. "His death was devastating for her. However, she seemed stronger than me back then in the early days. Now I believe she put her feelings on hold to be supportive of me. She didn't go for counseling, as she didn't feel she needed to. We attended survivors-of-suicide support group meetings together, but only because I asked her to.

"Numbed by my own grief, I truly never saw how she hid hers—through drinking. Today she is an alcoholic. Two years ago, my husband and I took her daughter away from her to live with us because most of the time she was too drunk to raise her. We hoped this would cause Kerry to seek help for her problems. But her drinking has only gotten worse. When she drinks, I don't know her. When she is sober, she is the sweet daughter I always knew. She dries out and is fine for a while. I pray constantly that one of these days she won't pick up that first drink after she has dried out."[2]

Surviving siblings also need to have a voice in making decisions so that they feel they are still part of the family structure. One survivor told us that she was totally left out of the decision-making process after her brother died. "If anyone would have listened," she said, "I could have given good input regarding his funeral and memorial service and what he would have wanted done." Brothers and sisters usually know each other better than their parents know them because of all their "don't tell Mom and Dad" secrets and the times of vulnerability they have shared.

The Grief of Siblings

The New Testament book of John recounts the grief of Mary and Martha when their brother, Lazarus, who was a friend of Jesus, died. When Jesus arrived, he was so deeply moved and troubled over the grief of Mary and Martha that he wept. The words used to describe this indicate that Jesus wept with gut-wrenching sobs, even though he knew that he would soon raise Lazarus to life (see John 11:1–44).

The grief that you feel over the loss of your sibling will most likely move you to tears, even gut-wrenching sobs, and may bring up emotional reactions in you that you have never before experienced.

Common emotions and reactions for a surviving sibling include:

- Resentment that the importance (to you) of the loss of your sibling has not been acknowledged
- Loneliness and isolation
- Fear of mentioning to peers how the death occurred

- Inability to grieve or talk about your sibling and confusion about how to deal with your feelings
- Feeling upset that you weren't able to say goodbye
- Intense sadness because of the loss of the relationship with your sibling *and* your parents, if they have become immersed in and consumed by their own grief
- Guilt because you feel that something you said or did may have led to the suicide or that you could have prevented it
- Feeling you're wrong for wanting to get on with your life and feel happy again
- Angry with God for allowing the suicide to happen

The Challenge of Overprotective Parents

Afraid of what may happen to their surviving children, parents often become overprotective and worry obsessively about their safety, especially worrying (though they rarely express it) that a surviving child may also take his own life. Ann said that her daughter was a year old when her son, Wayne, took his life. "She misses him, but it doesn't seem as much these days. In the beginning, she would go to his bedroom door and bang on it, saying, 'Way, Way.'

"I'm so worried about explaining his death to her as she grows up. I don't know how or even where to begin. It breaks my heart to think that she'll grow up knowing Wayne from visits to the cemetery and only by our shared stories, pictures, and videos. I hope she will have some memories of him and how they chased each other around and how they loved each other so much.

"I also worry about my reactions when she reaches age sixteen and if I'll be paranoid or overprotective because of Wayne's death at that age. I hope my husband and I can keep open the lines of communication with her and be able to talk freely about Wayne and his death. It doesn't need to be hidden or be something she should be afraid of."

I (Sue) was very concerned about my son, Steve, because the deaths of his sister and stepsister happened so close together and were followed by the death of his grandmother, just a few months after Shannon left us. The fact that Steve had been clinically depressed before Shannon died was an added factor in my

FINDING YOUR WAY

Find a support group if possible. Some communities have groups specifically for surviving siblings, which may meet at the same time as other groups for survivors of suicide.

Enlist allies. Though this chapter is addressed primarily to surviving siblings, with younger children, it is often up to the parents to creatively enlist all the allies they can find, for there is an enemy of their surviving children who would like to steal their hope and joy, day by day. After Josh's suicide, Debbie contacted her other children's schools and teachers. "We sent out a letter to the parents stating that a suicide had happened and that our children may need and want to talk about it. Jake's teacher had the class write letters to him. They were very supportive and loving, which meant a lot to Jake. When Brittany returned to school, there was a single rose on her desk. We felt that because of the response by the teachers and students, our children had a much easier time dealing with their brother's death."

concern. However, most siblings we have spoken with have said that the suicide of their brother or sister was actually a deterrent to their ever considering their own suicide. They could see firsthand the devastation it caused their families and decided they would never put their families through that again.

Toward Resolution

When your sibling chose death over life, many things were left unsaid. You might consider writing down your thoughts in the form of a letter to the deceased, even though you know she will never actually read it. What you do with the letter when it is finished is a personal choice. Some have offered their letter as a sacrifice of pain and forgiveness by burning it. You may choose to

Look for the positives that may emerge from your experience. As a surviving sibling, you may find that:

· You develop more compassion and understanding toward others than you had before your sibling's death.

· Your life goals and direction change; many survivors have become helping professionals.

· You no longer take things for granted.

· You value relationships with family, friends, and possibly God more than before.

If your parents seem overprotective, assure them that you appreciate their concern but that you also need them to trust you to make responsible choices. Tell them that when you are away from them, you know that you represent them, and you would never do anything to dishonor them. Promise them that you would never deliberately do anything to hurt them the way the death of your sibling has hurt them. Thank them for loving you enough to give you freedom to become who you hope to become.

bury the letter at your sibling's gravesite or at some other meaningful place. If you live near the ocean, you might seal your letter in a bottle and let the tides wash away your pain.

We began this chapter with one example, provided by Monica, one of our most faithful helpers in this project and one of your journey mates, whose brother DJ took his own life at age twenty. We end it with another, written by Steve to his sister, Shannon, who took her life at age nineteen:

Dear Shannon,

I know it's been a while since I have written. I've been really busy, working and building up my career. It's hard work you know, hoping for a family one day. A lot of things you have to do to be prepared.

So what's new with you? I haven't heard from you since you left. Hope all is good. So did you finish college? I know you were dying to be an architect—how's that going? Fallen in love yet? If so, I would love to meet him, and of course my nieces and nephews as well. (I can always hope can't I?)

I can't believe it has been almost thirteen years since we talked. Time flies when you're having fun. It hasn't seemed fun. I guess I could have done more to keep in touch. But after you left there were so many things you left behind, I didn't know where to begin. Mom was upset (and she had reason to be). I know you guys had your problems, but I think you could have worked through them. And Dad . . . well, he misses you a whole bunch. I catch him crying sometimes. You know he loves you, right? Well, he does . . . a lot.

And for me, well, I just didn't understand. I don't want to bring up old issues here but, well, you hurt a lot of people by leaving, and I just wish you could tell me your reasons. I won't judge you in any way—you know I never did that. But I just wish I knew your reasons. I hope I didn't do anything to encourage you to leave. That would devastate me. But if I did please let me know. I am a big boy now. I think I can handle what you might have to say.

I just want you home. We used to have fun as a family. I know not everything was peaches and cream. But if you came back, I know we could all have fun again. Well, I think I have said enough. I don't want to overwhelm you and have you think that I hate you or something, 'cause I don't. I love you, Shannon, and always will. You're my sister, and I just want you back in my life. Well, write me back when you can, and I will hopefully talk to you soon.

Your little brother,
Steve

Tears of My Heart

Lord, so many times
I've cried,
Why did you let
My daughter die?

Where were you?
Didn't you see?
What were you thinking?
Surely not of me.

Are you really good?
It's what I've been taught
And should I trust you?
I surely think not.

Doubt and mistrust
Our relationship awry
The chasm grows wider
With every "Why?"

My wounded heart pleads,
Father, I need your grace
Is my peace found in you
Or in some other place . . .

Where the heart knows no anguish
The spirit is blessed
With certain knowledge
My child is at rest?

Then I remember
I can stay or can flee
But I would be lost
If you ever left me.

—SUE FOSTER[1]

CHAPTER 9

Questions That Remain

For survivors who are believers, questions related to faith may linger for years. Resolving such questions complicates the grieving process because not only must one grieve an unbearable loss, but a believer must also be reconciled with a God who, for his own unknowable reasons, has allowed the unthinkable to happen to someone for whom his Word claims he loved enough to send his own Son to die.[2] It's a "love you, hate you, but there's no where else to turn" dilemma of colossal proportions, even if it does occur primarily within the hidden places of the heart. This extended inquiry often results in deeper, more realistic and authentic faith, but it does not always resolve as positively as uninformed observers might expect.

Where Were You, God?

Many survivors have cried, "Where were you, God?" Another way to ask this is, "Why didn't you prevent it from happening?"

Kathie said she'd like to ask God why he didn't make the gun jam.

Terri wrote, "I struggled with God, wondering where he was as I tried to talk Jack out of ending his life, but in hindsight, I realized he was there with me providing the words I spoke. I told Jack that God would love and forgive him *no matter what*—somehow providing forgiveness for the final act of his life."

The sense that God abandoned you and your family when he was most needed can result in disappointment and even anger with God. One survivor wrote: "I found myself mad at God for allowing this to happen to me and my

Finding Your Way

Emotions such as being angry with God are expressed in the Bible (see the stories of Job and Jonah, for example). But modern Christians don't have many categories in their neat systems of theology into which such emotions fit. Perhaps this is because modern-day believers are so focused on knowing *about* God, intellectually, that they can't imagine having such an intimate relationship with their Creator that expressing one's deepest hopes and hurts is a natural part of knowing and being known. They think, and they say, in one way or another: "A true believer should not—some might say *cannot*—be angry with God." By implication, if you are angry with God, you must not be a true believer.

Yet the real implication of Judy T.'s admission, and the foundation of the hope that her relationship with God will not only recover but become deeper than ever before, is that she believes in a God who desires truth in the inner being, especially when one's relationship with him has been damaged.[3]

By contrast, French existentialist philosopher Simone de Beauvoir said, "I cannot be angry at God, in whom I do not believe."

Many believers who experience affliction are surprised, disappointed, confused, bewildered, offended, and yes, sometimes

family. At the same time, I was praying to him to help us through this. When things like this happen, people try to tell you that God is perfect in all his ways. I have not been able to find anything good in what my family and I have gone through. I have heard of people who say, 'God has his reasons and I accept that, so it won't hurt me anymore, so I can go on with my life and not be unhappy.' I am not one of those people. In fact, I have never met anyone who could do that. I questioned my faith and my belief systems. I found it is a lot easier to talk

even angry that the God they love and who claims to love them
has allowed the situation that brought their suffering. Though
their Christian friends may not understand or approve, our
perspective is that the depth of their feeling of rejection or
abandonment or betrayal is directly proportional to the depth
of their love for God.

So if you are experiencing any of these sentiments toward
God, we urge you to be frank and honest with him, for he
knows about it anyway, and he's neither surprised nor, in our
opinion, offended by such confessions. Our observation is that
many believers who are willing to risk such open communication follow up their admission with, "But I'm sure glad you're
with me, for you're all I have."

While the more theological among your friends may insist
you must repent—in dust and ashes, à la Job—(and perhaps
even be witnessed by another human) in order for forgiveness
and reconciliation with God to occur, we take heart from the
parable of the Prodigal Son. Upon his return, the son began to
confess his sins, but the father (representing God in this story)
did not let him finish but embraced and welcomed him home
(see Luke 15:21-24). Your heavenly Father already knows your
heart and your words before you speak them. Entrust your
deepest feelings to him, and then listen with your heart for his
response.

about death and loss of loved ones in the abstract than it is to actually deal with
the experience."

Judy T. wrote, "Because my husband is a minister and a small group of powerful leaders in our Episcopal church turned on him after our daughter's suicide, God ceased to even exist for me. It was like being alone in a dark, black
hole. I knew there was light, but I also knew that if I was going to get back into
the light, I was going to have to climb up alone. People gave me safe hugs or

listened to me and helped me find words of strength, but *all* the work had to be done for me, by me. It was a totally lonely time.

"Not until I was in London sometime later did I again have the sense that God was there—at Evensong in Westminster Abbey, after a day of touring the Tower of London. It wasn't until two years later, however, that I finally heard a song that gave faith a context that made any sense. 'Gone from mystery on to mystery,' said the lyrics, 'gone from darkness into light; a little bit closer to the darkness, closer to the light.'⁴ Those words made it all make sense. The net result is that I am still angry with God, but there is some comfort in having God to be angry at."

Where Is My Loved One Now?

In far too many cases, the church has not only failed to love and support survivors in their time of grief; it has seriously hindered and delayed their healing as well. By "church" in this case, we mean not only the institution by that name but also the individuals who are part of it. Their most hurtful hindrance is the suggestion that the deceased loved one is in hell because suicide is unforgivable.

Lucy, whose mother took her own life, wrote: "I felt that God held me responsible for my mother's suicide. This message was corroborated by church practice, such as refusing to bury my mother's body in hallowed ground and booting me from Brownies and Sunday school. But over time," she added, "I figured out that God, who created the human capacity for love, couldn't possibly have wanted church policymakers and leaders to behave this way, so I left the Christian church. But I continue to pray and to acknowledge God daily in all that is good and possible about being human."

The example of Lucy's church echoes medieval practices and is surely not aligned with the law of love that Jesus entrusted to his followers. Such attitudes and practice have no biblical basis. Jesus, who would not break off a bruised reed or snuff out a flickering wick (see Matt. 12:20), would never treat a survivor of suicide this way. Moreover, he would tell this religious organization that neither their church property nor their cemetery is "hallowed ground" owned by them but that the whole earth is hallowed ground, created and owned by God himself.

You'll recall the story of Jenny, whose daughter died of a self-inflicted gunshot wound. As if the rejection she experienced from some Christian friends wasn't enough, she received a letter from her brother, a Baptist minister, saying: "I can't absolve her; you'll have to accept that she's probably in hell."

The outrageous statement of Jenny's brother has three flaws, the first being that Jenny "will have to accept" such heartless nonsense. She should only accept what is true in light of the Scriptures.

Second, the phrase "I can't absolve her," though technically true—he can't absolve *anyone*—is unusual for most Protestant ministers. In the reformed theology of Lutherans, Presbyterians, Baptists, Pentecostals, and others, only God has the power to absolve a person's sins (*ab* means "from"; *solvere* means "to free"). The idea that any mediator other than Christ Jesus,[5] our advocate with the Father,[6] must be involved for absolution to occur is based in Roman Catholic theology. Absolution is the pardoning of sin, and its punishment is prescribed by a priest, following a person's confession.[7]

Third, the idea that Jenny's daughter is in hell is presumptuous, judgmental beyond this man's ability to know, and is another holdover from Roman Catholic dogma.[8] That belief is partly based on the idea that since suicide cannot be followed by confession to and absolution by a representative of the church, the sin of suicide, therefore, is not forgivable.

In early Christianity, suicide was sometimes regarded as a virtuous act. Eusebius, in his account of the martyrs at Antioch, told of a mother and two daughters who drowned themselves in a river to avoid being raped.[9]

A few centuries later, Augustine argued that the women were wrong to assume that rape would necessarily have deprived them of their purity, because purity is a state of mind—a rather Aristotelian concept at best. Christians choosing martyrdom through one means or another was a problem to a church interested in increasing its constituency, so Augustine's bottom line was that since at no point does the Bible sanction taking one's life, he decreed that "Thou shalt not kill" applies to one's own life as well as to the lives of others. Augustine's teachings on the subject became church doctrine.

Throughout the Middle Ages, those who attempted suicide were flogged, imprisoned, and stripped of all social and financial assets. Those whose attempts were successful had their corpses publicly desecrated, their memories defamed, and their property confiscated. Surviving families were left ostracized and destitute.

Thirteenth-century theologian Thomas Aquinas reasoned: "To bring death upon oneself in order to escape the other afflictions of this life is to adopt a greater evil in order to avoid a lesser. . . . Suicide is the most fatal of sins because it cannot be repented of."[10]

Martin Luther is reported to have said privately, in his "Table Talk" of April 7, 1532: "I don't share the opinion that suicides are certainly to be damned. My reason is that they do not wish to kill themselves but are overcome by the power of the devil. They are like a man who is murdered in the woods by a robber. However, this ought not to be taught to the common people, lest Satan be given an opportunity to cause slaughter."[11]

The only major theological work in defense of suicide for about twelve hundred years was by the famous English poet and cleric John Donne, whose work *Biathanatos* was not published until 1647, sixteen years after his death. Donne wrote, "Whensoever any affliction assails me, me thinks I have the keys of my prison in mine own hand, and no remedy presents itself so soon to my heart, as mine own sword."

The Westminster Shorter Catechism (seventeenth century), which remains authoritative for Calvinists, says: "The sixth commandment forbiddeth the taking away of our own life, or the life of our neighbor unjustly, or whatsoever tendeth thereunto." In general, the Reformers adopted and carried forward the teachings of the Roman Catholic Church.

Desecration of the corpses of those who took their own lives and confiscation of their estates was not abolished in England until 1823. Only as recently as 1961 did England repeal its law making attempted suicide a crime. Canada followed suit in 1972. As recently as 1974, attempting suicide was still a crime in nine states in the United States.

Considering even this short historical overview, perhaps it should not astound us to find that the punitive and judgmental attitudes toward suicide reflected in the comments and actions reported above are still alive and thriving. However, since many of today's evangelical churches proclaim the Bible as their only source of truth, the crucial question is: What does the Bible have to say about suicide? And the answer to that question is: Not very much.

The Bible neither condemns nor condones suicide, unless you insist that the sixth of the Ten Commandments, "Thou shalt not kill," means you shall not kill (or murder, with premeditation—the more common meaning of the Hebrew word used here) your own self. But the true meaning of any biblical text is not determined by what we want it to mean; it is understood by trying to discern the author's original intention, considering the context in which the text occurs. In this case, God, through Moses, most likely is forbidding the Israelites to take the law into their own hands by murdering their neighbors, whether in revenge or for any other reason. Surely this command was not a general prohibition against killing anyone, since the Israelites, with God's blessing, killed plenty of their enemies after they received the commandments. Nor does it seem to apply to suicide.

The Bible speaks of seven self-killings, one attempted suicide (Jonah, who threw himself overboard, only to be swallowed by the great fish and delivered to Nineveh), a suggestion that suicide might be a good idea in order to end the pain (Job's wife suggested this to her husband), and one thwarted suicide (the Philippian jailer who thought that Paul and Silas had escaped). Perhaps the best-known account of suicide is that of Judas, who hanged himself after he betrayed Jesus.

In the Old Testament, Israel's first king, Saul, fell on his sword rather than be taken captive in battle. His armor-bearer did the same (1 Sam. 31:1–6). The book of Judges describes how Samson pushed against the pillars supporting the temple of the god Dagon and shouted, "Let me die with the Philistines!" (16:30). When the building fell, Samson, and many of his enemies, died. The other three biblical suicides were minor Old Testament figures. (See 2 Sam. 17:23; 1 Kings 16:18–19; Judg. 9:52–54.)

Perhaps the most pertinent thing to our subject in relation to these accounts is that the biblical writers do not condemn the suicides. In fact, Samson is listed as a hero of faith in the New Testament book of Hebrews. And Saul was honored by David, likely the author of the psalm of lament composed for Saul, found in 2 Samuel 1:24–25.

The fact that suicide is not condemned in Scripture does not mean, however, that it is condoned. Otherwise, why would Paul and Silas have remained behind in the prison, preventing their jailer from killing himself? Nor through this analysis are we condoning suicide. Our point is that where the Bible is silent, it is better to admit that we do not know what God has not revealed.

We are, however, certain of one thing. Suicide is not the unpardonable sin that some have made it; Dante, following the lead of Aquinas, consigned suicides to the lowest place in hell. But Jesus said, "Every sin and blasphemy will be forgiven men, but the blasphemy against the Spirit will not be forgiven" (Matt. 12:31).

Nor are we universalists, in the sense that we think *every* person, no matter how or in what spiritual state he or she may die, goes to heaven. The Scriptures are clear in saying we are saved by grace, through faith in Jesus Christ,[12] who paid the penalty for our sins and who said that no one comes to the Father except through him.[13]

Further, we are not using the term "saved" in the sense sometimes employed in the modern evangelical church, which often links "becoming saved" with walking the aisle to the altar, or raising one's hand in a service (with every head bowed and every eye closed), or praying a prayer at the end of a booklet. We are saved by grace through faith, and even the ability to believe is a gift from God, unrelated to our works, lest anyone should boast (Eph. 2:8–9). Therefore, the entire matter is between an individual and God, who understands troubled hearts and confused minds better than any human ever will.

The interchange of faith between a person and God occurs on a soul level, and it can occur in the very last minutes or seconds or split seconds of a person's mortal life, when the Holy Spirit intercedes with the Father through groanings because words cannot express the sense of futility and despair when all a person can think is, *God, I can't go on* (Rom. 8:26–27). This can be a cry of faith, not defiance; of weakness, not pride; of humility, not arrogance. It is a cry that, in light of all God has revealed about himself, he honors.[14]

What Difference Does Faith Make?

Survivors for whom faith is nonexistent or irrelevant have only the deceased, fate, or other factors to blame for their loss. They may hurl their lament toward an empty sky or howl it into an empty chasm, but for most such mourners, self-

FINDING YOUR WAY

Do not be surprised if someone suggests that your deceased loved one is in hell, for this type of thinking still permeates the church, even though such thinking has no biblical basis. There is probably no point in engaging such a person in dialogue about this matter, nor is it healthy for you, emotionally or spiritually, to become bitter as a result. As much as possible, emulate the Lord, who prayed for his executioners: "Father, forgive them, for they do not know what they are doing" (Luke 23:34). Even if the sixth commandment, "Thou shalt not kill," does apply to suicide, many who have killed—whether others or themselves—have been saved by faith.

Place your confidence in a God who knows that your loved one was deeply troubled and perhaps beyond the reach of reason at the end. No one can know what kind of dialogue occurred between God and your loved one during those last few seconds or split seconds. Since God is light (and moves at the speed of light), in a situation such as this, time can stand still for necessary communication to occur.

Commit yourself, as much as possible, to a life of faithfulness, which will in the end bring you to eternity with the Lord and with your loved one, if he or she really was one of his.

preservation eventually takes over and they choose to get on with life, painful as it may be and pointless as it may seem. In the secular understanding of stages of grief, this is called "acceptance." But in reality, it is only resignation.

Faith—authentic faith—is the only possible context of actual resolution of your grief following the suicide of someone you love. It is the key to discovering meaning and purpose where there seemed to be none. When it combines our pain with God's power, it is the catalyst that can result in ministry to others and in an opportunity to witness to a world that desperately needs to know that God is real and *now here* instead of *nowhere*.

We used the words "authentic faith" because there is a certain type of shallower faith that seems adequate when things are good but is insufficient when bad things happen to good people. Perhaps you've heard someone give a testimony in church about how glad she is that she "got saved" during an evangelistic "revival" meeting some time ago. Now the primary focus of her faith is that she looks forward to going to heaven when she dies. This is sad, because it implies that for that person, at least, whatever happened long ago is the beginning and end of their faith.

True faith is not an eternal life insurance policy without relevance to today's realities. It's not an invitation to "the good life." It's not a guarantee of a life free of trouble, worry, pain, sorrow, or suffering, but an invitation to trust in the promises of God, wherever that leads. For the Old Testament heroes of faith, it meant that some "were tortured and refused to be released, so that they might gain a better resurrection. Some faced jeers and flogging, while still others were chained and put in prison. They were stoned; they were sawed in two; they were put to death by the sword. They went about in sheepskins and goatskins, destitute, persecuted and mistreated—the world was not worthy of them. They wandered in deserts and mountains, and in caves and holes in the ground. These were all commended for their faith, yet none of them received what had been promised. God had planned something better for us so that only together with us would they be made perfect" (Heb. 11:35–40).

For the New Testament heroes of faith, and for all the other martyrs through the ages since then, authentic faith was the same—often with similar results. The persecution continues today; in some places in the world at this moment, it is dangerous to be known as a follower of Christ.

Authentic faith is, according to Hebrews 11:1, "the substance [reality] of things hoped for, the evidence [proof] of things not seen" (KJV). We prefer the translation of the King James Version for this passage because it is more or less word for word from the original Greek. The New International Version reads, "Now faith is being sure of what we hope for and certain of what we do not see." The point in either case is that people with authentic faith "see," with the eyes of faith, supernatural realities. These realities include the fact that God, the Creator of the universe, really does exist, and he rewards those who diligently seek him (Heb. 11:3, 6). Believers who have authentic faith are so confident of these realities that they are willing to die rather than deny them.

Authentic faith is dynamic—a living, breathing, personal, relational experience with the Almighty, with whom an ongoing dialogue is possible. Sometimes this dialogue is as simple as: "Lord, help," with the response being, "Do not be afraid; I am with you. Do not be anxious; I am *for* you." Or, in the words of Jesus, "These things I have spoken unto you, that in me ye might have peace. In the world ye shall have tribulation: but be of good cheer; I have overcome the world" (John 16:33 KJV). This is one statement of Christ's that most believers would like to edit. But the truth is that in this world, we do have tribulation.

So, back to the question: What difference does faith make?

Answer: All the difference between despair and hope, futility and meaning, chaos and purpose, death and life. Despair, futility, chaos, and death are the Devil's realm, for he was a liar, deceiver, and murderer from the beginning (John 8:44). Hope, meaning, purpose, and life—in fact, life more abundantly—all originate in the kingdom of God, the supernatural realm, which only eyes of faith can see.

If faith only matters in the good times, then it doesn't matter very much. But the Scriptures are clear that faith is tested and proven, refined and purified, primarily through affliction. Note the following Bible passages.

> But he knows the way that I take; when he has tested me, I will come forth as gold.
>
> —JOB 23:10

> Therefore, since we have been justified through faith, we have peace with God through our Lord Jesus Christ, through whom we have gained access by faith into this grace in which we now stand. And we rejoice in the hope of the glory of God. Not only so, but we also rejoice in our sufferings, because we know that suffering produces perseverance; perseverance, character; and character, hope. And hope does not disappoint us, because God has poured out his love into our hearts by the Holy Spirit, whom he has given us.
>
> —ROMANS 5:1–5

> Consider it pure joy, my brothers, whenever you face trials of many kinds, because you know that the testing of your faith develops perseverance.

Perseverance must finish its work so that you may be mature and complete, not lacking anything.

—JAMES 1:2–4

In this you greatly rejoice, though now for a little while you may have had to suffer grief in all kinds of trials. These have come so that your faith—of greater worth than gold, which perishes even though refined by fire—may be proved genuine and may result in praise, glory and honor when Jesus Christ is revealed.

—1 PETER 1:6–7

Assuming that these passages are true and trustworthy, believers ought not be surprised by suffering but, when it comes, try to discover what God is trying to teach them and where he seems to want to take them through the refining of their faith. These are not easy things to discern, especially right after a tragedy, when most of us would trade *any* amount of personal growth just to have our loved one back again. It is only natural to ask "Why? Why? Why?" as in "What did I do to deserve this?" or "I demand an explanation!" But the route to healing comes when we begin to ask the question another way: "Lord, help me understand how such a thing as this can possibly be part of your plan for me and for the one who has died."

This question assumes something about God that is absolutely true: In everything he causes or allows, he is motivated by love for those who are his and the advancement of his purposes (both present and eternally). Since his ways are not our ways, nor are his thoughts ours (Isa. 55:8), it is highly unlikely that in any given situation that brings human sorrow, anyone can say for sure why God has caused or allowed it to happen. But we can know beyond any doubt that he is not capricious, uninvolved, or even indifferent to our pain.

As Dave wrote, "the truth is, pain has *two faces*, human *and* divine. The human face is haggard, drawn, contorted, and streaked with tears. The divine is calm, assuring, kind, and loving—and likewise streaked with tears."[15]

One of the greatest paradoxes of faith is this: sometimes life is abominable, but a loving God is in control. Suffering has two sides. God never asks us to deny our pain, for that would be a lie. And he doesn't ask us to enjoy it, for that would be masochism. All he asks is that we surrender our pain to him and then watch him transform it into something else.

Jesus understands and cares, as this passage affirms: "For we have not an high priest [Jesus] which cannot be touched with the feeling of our infirmities; but was in all points tempted like as we are, yet without sin. Let us therefore come boldly unto the throne of grace, that we may obtain mercy, and find grace to help in time of need" (Heb. 4:15–16 KJV).

And because Jesus understands and cares, he is the only true source of healing. "He was despised and rejected by men," the prophet Isaiah wrote, "a man of sorrows, and familiar with suffering. Like one from whom men hide their faces he was despised, and we esteemed him not. Surely he took up our infirmities and carried our sorrows, yet we considered him stricken by God, smitten by him, and afflicted. But he was pierced for our transgressions, he was crushed for our iniquities; the punishment that brought us peace was upon him, and by his wounds we are healed" (Isa. 53:3–5).

FINDING YOUR WAY

When you are willing to risk it, entrust your very self—all you are, have been, and ever will be (the good, the bad, the ugly, and everything in between)—into the hands of a God who loves you enough to let his own Son die in your place. You can trust him. He can and will heal you if you ask him to show you how to work with him to redeem the whole journey, good and bad, happy and sad, for his purposes and glory. To the degree that you do this, those around you who don't know him or even believe that he exists will demand to know the reason for the hope that is in you (1 Peter 3:15). The mere fact that you continue to walk in faith despite what has happened irrefutably demonstrates "the substance [reality] of things hoped for, the evidence [proof] of things not seen" (Heb. 11:1 KJV). As a result, you will not have to seek opportunities for ministry; as you keep walking by faith, opportunities for ministry will come to you.

How This Works Out in Real Life

Linda wrote: "My faith in a loving God has sustained me throughout the entire experience. I have sensed his presence and leading in my life. He has been faithful through (what I hope is) the worst experience of my life, and I know that he will continue to keep me in the palm of his hand—no matter what happens to me. If anything, my faith has grown, and I feel a stronger sense of God's presence in my life.

"When my son, Paul, took his own life in June 1993, I suddenly found myself on a very dark road, with no light and no roadmap. Having no frame of reference in my life for surviving a suicide death, I faced a complicated and difficult healing process. When some time had passed, the initial anesthetizing patch of fog lifted, and my brain began to function again. I realized that God was not only providing light, love, and guidance for my journey, but he had also lovingly equipped me to walk that treacherous road.

"Five years before Paul's death, I had experienced a divorce—after twenty-six years of marriage. God graciously provided me with an extensive divorce recovery education. Among other things, I learned to gradually let go of a relationship and to accept the loss of future dreams. I learned how to grieve and to experience and express all of my God-given emotions in an adult, moderate way. I learned to practice forgiveness—for others and for myself. I learned to take responsibility and ownership of my life. I learned that I had no control over the choices of others and no responsibility for the consequences of their behavior. I learned to connect with safe people in healthy relationships and how to ask for their help without shame or guilt. And, most importantly, I learned to fully experience God's presence and to hold on tight to my inherent value as his beloved child in the midst of rejection and abandonment. With God's help, a lot of hard work, two support groups, and a host of encouraging friends and family members, I survived that divorce and did a great deal of growing up in the process.

"All of those lessons provided me with just the right tools to survive and overcome an even more incomprehensible loss, and also to share that experience with others in order to shed the light of God's love on their dark path. That's what I call 'a God thing'—because I certainly could not have done any of it in my own strength!

"Ten years after Paul's suicide, my life is back on track—a much different track than I ever imagined, but I have a strong sense that God has me right where he wants me. With God's help, I have been able to reclaim the joy that was lost when Paul died. He (and his death) will always be a part of my history, but they're not *all* of my history, like they were in the first few years after he died. God has made me stronger and more confident than I was before Paul died. This has made it possible to share my experience with others and to work to prevent suicides and hopefully spare others the experience of living in the aftermath of a suicide death."[16]

Both of us (Dave and Sue) have also experienced the remarkable power of God to redeem our journey through and beyond our deepest sorrows and to transform it into help for others. I (Dave) would never have chosen to focus my ministry efforts on such things as recovery from losses, depression, or suicide, but before I was born, the Lord knew the way I would take. When I have chosen to keep walking by faith, he has walked with me. When I have been unfaithful, he, like the father of the Prodigal Son, has waited for me to come back to my senses. Then he has invited me to continue on toward the fulfillment of the purpose for which he keeps me here.

For me (Sue), the journey has also had its twists and turns. There were times after Shannon died when I was angry at God and railed at him. There were times when I was tempted to walk away because I didn't see how this fit with his being a good and just God. However, my daughter's death and all other times of great loss have strengthened my faith and have drawn me closer to him. Somehow I just knew that if I held on and didn't give up, he would bring me through the pain and adversity, and he has never failed to do this.

While I still wonder why God allowed Shannon to die, I don't struggle any longer with finding purpose or meaning in it. I never would have thought that I would be as involved in the whole area of suicide as I am now. I truly believe this is the "beauty out of ashes" that God intended from this tragedy. He just keeps opening more doors, and for now at least, this is the ministry he intends for me.

Keep Breathing

Sometimes it feels like the sun will never rise
Like the birds will never sing again
The night is dark, not one star in the sky
and no one you can call a friend
In so deep
It feels like you are drowning
So afraid
You can hardly catch your breath

Keep breathing
Take it in and let it out
Keep breathing
It's gonna be OK
Believe in
A power greater than what you are going through
When you don't know what to do, keep breathing

You know the one that reaches through the hurt
A comfort for the broken heart
But in this place even prayers are painful
Life isn't s'posed to be this hard
When relief is more than you can hope for
And the wounds seem deeper than your faith

CHORUS

Don't give up
Even though you want to
Don't give in
You've already come this far
It's alright
The Lord knows what you're needing
And he'll meet you where you are,
just . . . keep breathing.

CHORUS

—SCOTT KRIPPAYNE AND STEVE SILER*

CHAPTER 10

Survival — and Beyond

Before the suicide, you were just a regular person with hopes and dreams like most other regular people. But suddenly you became a "survivor of suicide." Suicide chose you, and not the reverse, bringing with it chaos and heartache and pain you thought would never end — hurt so intense that at times you may have considered joining your loved one. But you didn't. You're still here, surviving, and that's a good thing.

Things Are Different Now

You can't go back. The suicide of your loved one changed everything. But you may wonder, *Will it always be this way? Will it ever be possible to do more than just barely survive each day? Will I ever laugh again, be happy — really live again?*

Possibly not. Some people get stuck in their grief, so their epitaph reads, "Died at 50; buried at 70."

But this epitaph is not inevitable for survivors of suicide. You can move forward. We're not going to burden you with false expectations. We won't use terms like "victors versus victims" or other trite phrases that imply that if you have the right kind of faith, or courage, or resilience, or whatever, you should be able to rise above this trial and somehow leave it all behind.

As you survive, you move with your grief, through it, and beyond it, even to the point of learning to use the lessons you've learned and the character you've gained to help others who are on a similar path. You cannot make this happen in your own strength. To be real and effective, this must be a work of God, who is more powerful than anything the Evil One can bring or has brought your way. God is able to align even the most dreadful tragedy with his primary purpose, which is redemption.

Louise Wirick, who lost her twenty-seven-year-old son, Rob, to suicide in 1998, wrote: "Often, as a survivor, we feel like the pain is so intense and so permanent that we will never laugh or have a good life again. This isn't true, so please hold on tight to your hope that things will get better for you. I was so sure that I would never laugh again, or even smile a sincere smile again, after my son's death.

"I can now tell you that I have reclaimed my life. It was the hardest thing I have ever done, and I had many days that I struggled with thoughts of joining my son because I knew I could not live with that unbearable pain for the rest of my life. I just didn't believe it would ever get better.

"For those of you that are in that place now, please trust me when I say that it is not a permanent thing. You, too, will come to a day, very slowly, where you will begin to feel a little of that 'old you' come alive again, and hope will slowly begin to spring up. It's a slow process, for healing is just that—a process. We have so many issues to work through and come to a peace with: the why's, that horrendous guilt that seems to have a choke hold on so many of us at first, and the many, many unanswered questions.

"There seems to be a time that it is all replayed over and over, like we can somehow make the ending different by reliving it all, by reexamining every little detail. We have a rewind button in our minds, but not in real life, so we continue to come to the same questions with no one to give answers. But in doing so, although we don't know it at the time, we also slowly come to a peace with it by going through this process. For some, the peace comes in knowing that we will just never know and we have to accept that. For others, pieces will fit together and bring you answers that will suffice.

"I just want to encourage you that one day you will look back and be amazed at the progress you have made. I couldn't see it at all until I looked back on it later. I felt like I was spinning my wheels, but I wasn't. And the day my vision cleared enough for me to see, I was really amazed. It felt good!

"The day we were hurled into this nightmare, we were victims. We had no choice in it. But if we stay victims it's by choice. We have to learn how to be survivors and even more than survivors. You can do this! It's a hard battle, but life is hard . . . so what's new? Hard does not mean it isn't doable."[1]

What Does Survival Look Like?

Linda Flatt told us that for her, "survival is a place where my loss is not 'in my face' all the time, a place where there are many, many more good days than bad, and a place where I know that my life has moved forward in spite of my son's suicide. Survival is also a place of memories of Paul — and tears because I miss him. But the memories and tears are a *part* of who I am now, not *all* of who I am. Survival is a place of reclaimed joy and hope. With God's help and the help of my supportive and loving family and friends, I feel I have (thankfully) survived very well."

Survival is not moving on and forgetting about your loved one, as if to put all that you've experienced behind you forever, for you couldn't do that even if you tried. What has happened is now a part of who you are, not just part of your experience. C. S. Lewis once wrote about how we carry forward memories of our loved ones in our minds, which are a part of our soul that lives on into eternity. In this special sense, all your loved ones who have preceded you in death, even when their means of doing so was suicide, live on — within your mind. They also live on in the form of their own eternal souls.

As a survivor, you will continue to have painful memories and reminders of what happened. You may struggle with anniversary dates. You will cry and experience other painful emotions when you think of your loved one. And these responses to your memories may continue for the rest of your life. There's no right or wrong about this. As you move through and beyond your grief, you will eventually have more good days than bad days. The memories will be less painful — even more pleasant — over time. And the emotions will be much more manageable.

I (Dave) recall how for a long time after Jonathan died, I thought of him every day, and when I did, my main emotion was gut-wrenching pain and sorrow beyond words as I thought of what had happened and, even more, about what might have been. It all seemed like some kind of cosmic joke, or perhaps more like a riddle about futility that I would never understand. It was hard for me to even look at his photo, impossible to listen to tapes or to view home movies. Dreams die hard. Grief must be processed. You can't go around it, only through it.

I couldn't understand why a three-year-old with such promise had to die, and the way it happened seemed so cruel. But slowly, very slowly (whether too slowly only God can judge), my responses changed. When I thought of him—his personality, his laughter, his love for me—at some indefinable point in time, my response became more than pain, anger, self-pity, and remorse. Instead of feeling offended that God had taken Jonathan, I began to feel thankful that he had been a part of my life and love for even such a short time. Today as I write this, I'm looking at a picture of him. I feel a certain pressure in my chest and a shortness of breath, but I also see a blond-haired, blue-eyed boy who loved me, and still does—as I do, him. He lives on in my mind, and I know that we will be as we were, in what will seem, looking back, but a moment in time. Such a change—beyond survival—is the result of hope that is an anchor for our souls (Heb. 6:19), because it is linked to the promises of God, who is worthy of our trust.

Finding Hope

Through the prophet Jeremiah, God says, "I know the plans that I have for you, plans for welfare and not for calamity; to give you a future and a hope" (Jer. 29:11 NASB). I (Sue) remember when I first found that verse after Shannon died. I held on to it for dear life. Was it really possible that there could be a future, that purpose could be found in the pile of ashes that my life had been reduced to? Hope became the thread that tied my fragile life together. Since that awful day in 1991, God has shown me over and over that he can bring forth purpose and meaning out of the tragedy of Shannon's death.

While writing this chapter, a dear friend called regarding her daughter, who seemed very depressed and was talking about suicide. She wondered if this was something she should take seriously and, if so, what kind of help should she seek for her daughter. She sought psychiatric help, and her daughter benefited from a week in a psychiatric hospital. My friend later told me that if she hadn't known me, known my story, and taken seriously my advice to get help *now*, she probably would have brushed it aside as something her daughter was just going through and would probably get over on her own. We all know that the result of this inaction could have been deadly. In helping to prevent a possible tragedy, I found a sense of joy and gratitude. No, it didn't change the depth of my loss, but God used that loss to help someone else.

Grieving's timetable is as individual as you are. You can't "hurry up and get over it," nor can others push or pull you through it. And just as you have your own unique timetable for grief, you will have your own timetable for coming out of the grief. You will know when you are ready to move on.

The pain will lessen. You will actually be able to focus on things other than your deceased loved one and the circumstances surrounding the death. Activities and people that you used to enjoy will bring you joy again, and the intense emotions of anger, guilt, sadness, and depression will begin to subside.

You will begin looking forward to life again, though it will be without your loved one. As hope has kept you moving through the grief and pain, hope will drive your desire to live again.

How Does Hope Accomplish This Reconnection with Life?

We asked a few survivors to describe the dynamics of recovering the desire to live as they experienced them.

Debbie said, "You can get to a point in your grief, somewhere along the path, that you somehow see the beauty of your surroundings again. To me, that is new hope, a new step in your life. We have to grow, or we will be stuck in a time frame and the emotional turmoil forever. We have to find ways to cope with our loss each day. But when we can do this, there is hope we will find a different inner peace in our hearts and lives again."

"Hope is about having a reason to put one foot in front of the other and get on with my life," Linda wrote. "Thus, recovery, surviving, and hope are all part of the same package for me."

"I think we all need the hope that we'll find and thrive in the 'new normal,'" Terri wrote. "When we get to the point where we can rest in God's grace, we find eternal hope of seeing our loved one again. Finding hope is also knowing we are secure enough in our grief journey to reach behind us to help someone else."

Judy T. wrote, "Shortly after Lea died, hope was very small. But it has continued to grow. It was the only thing I had at first: hope that I could make some sense from the senseless. Hope for my other kids that we could each find our own paths that would lead us to life. At first, I had no hope that God had a plan. Going back to graduate school was a way of acting out my hope that some treasure could be found out of Lea's death that would make life possible for somebody else. Hope also took the form of the gift of love from all the other survivors, who I have found everywhere, and even the love from people who could see my hurt and were still willing and able to love me despite my brokenness. When hope got weak, I got angry, and the anger pushed me through to another level and then softened to hope again. Strong feelings, both good and bad, continued to remind me that I was alive and life hurt, but I knew that life was better than death."

Ginger wrote, "Hope is once again finding simple joys in life, something to hang on to, something to believe in. It's regaining the desire to live, not just exist. I believe that with hope comes purpose. Everyone needs a purpose in their life, to make it really worth living. We need hope to forge ahead, to believe that, yes, there is a light shining for us over the horizon. I believe it is God who is shining that light."

Becky wrote, "Survival to me is just being able to get through one day at a time and knowing that God has a reason for me still being here. For the most part, I do feel I have survived well. I am thankful for all the support I have received from family and friends. The only thing I might have done differently was to take a few more days off of work, but at the same time, I think going back earlier helped me get back to reality quicker. I know I was zoned out the first week or two and wasn't my normal cheerful self, but my life had been turned upside down. I think I pulled through as well as could be expected. I vowed to be more appreciative of everyone around me after going through the darkest days of my life and asked God continuously to keep me strong enough to do this. Recently I prayed to God to know the right words to say to a friend whose child had just taken her own life. I wanted to help her understand that she too could survive. I feel that through this all, I have become a more compassionate person with everyone."

People of the Heart

In more than twenty-five years of experiencing, and observing others experience, the journey from extreme loss to survival and beyond, I (Dave) have often witnessed pain being transformed into powerful ministry to others.

When you reach the point in your journey where your focus is as much (or more) on the needs of others than on your own loss and everything that came with it, it is one sure sign that you are moving beyond survival and becoming what I call a "person of the heart." Such people usually possess certain definable characteristics. People of the heart are:

- Authentic — speaking truth, asking and listening to the hardest questions
- Transparent — being open, not afraid to let others see inside
- Trusting — willing to live with the ambiguity of the riddle called life
- Dependent — centered on God instead of on anyone or anything else, yet also interdependent, needing others and being needed by them
- Forgiving — free from the need to get even because they've seen their own depravity and weaknesses
- Empowered — with supernatural strength because they know they are not strong enough by themselves
- Hopeful — even when despair seems more reasonable
- Humble — having a servant heart, willing to sacrifice for another's welfare
- Faithful — with spiritual eyes that see and embrace eternal realities and the earthly values that flow from them
- Peaceful — because all is in God's hands
- Joyful — having gone beyond mere happiness
- Patient — willing to wait for God and others
- Kind — willing to treat others as "kindred"
- Gentle — bruised reeds they do not break; flickering wicks they do not snuff out
- Tender — responsive to needs, without judgment
- Benevolent — merciful, caring for the down-and-out
- Generous — giving without keeping account

- Compassionate—able to feel others' pain in their hearts
- Loving—committed to the best interests of others as a result of intimacy with God

More often than not, people with these characteristics have been through the fire of suffering in one way or another. In other words, they are survivors, like you and us. And they are survivors who made a choice: to give their pain to God so he could turn it around and use it for good.

All people of the heart, including those whose brief stories follow, would want you to know two things:

1. There is nothing extraordinary about them; they're just trying to fulfill a sense of mission that grew out of their own long and often lonely journey.
2. Their ability to help their fellow strugglers didn't develop overnight but began with a willingness to be used, if possible, and then increased with experience and networking with others with similar interests.

If you wish to follow their lead, try to focus not on suicide itself or on the suicide of your loved one in particular but on survival and beyond, asking yourself what this would look like for you. It might mean a move to a new location, a new career, going back to school to finish that degree, a makeover into a "new you," volunteering in some capacity in your church or community, perhaps becoming more actively involved in a support group for survivors of suicide or in one of the several organizations you'll find listed in the resources section or those you'll read about shortly.

Whatever route you choose, you'll have to reach beyond your own walls when you are ready to do so. But don't rush yourself. Sometimes people who are grieving engage in a frenzy of activity before they are really ready—often on the advice of friends, family, or their church—with the result that all the noise and activity keeps them from feeling and working through their pain. When this is coupled with conforming to the pressures others place on them to do or say the "right" things, such as giving a testimony in church or representing God when they're still ambivalent toward him, the results can be emotionally and spiritually devastating. Rest . . . rest assured that God is not in nearly as much of a hurry as you or your friends may be in terms of this process.

Meet Members of the Hope Alliance

Mark Wilson's father shot himself on March 11, 1972, when Mark was seventeen. For ten years, his family didn't talk about it. During that time, Mark numbed his pain with drugs and alcohol. On November 2, 1981, he was introduced to Alcoholics Anonymous; he hasn't had a drink or used drugs since. In 1992, Mark started attending a suicide-survivor support group through the Baton Rouge Crisis Intervention Center, where he was able to talk about his father's suicide for the first time. This was a key to his healing and recovery. He now cofacilitates a suicide-survivor support group, has been involved with the Baton Rouge Crisis Intervention Center for over ten years, and is on the LOSS (Local Outreach to Suicide Survivors) team.

The LOSS team is a unique program in Baton Rouge whose purpose is to place trained survivors who are well along in the healing process at the scene of a suicide and in the presence of the family and friends, offering support and information right at the time of death or discovery. The team members help the family deal with all sorts of issues, including arranging for scene cleanup, helping with funeral details, acting as a buffer between the family and law enforcement, and so on. But mostly they provide very personal, intense support aimed at mitigating the devastation going on and getting the family and friends into pertinent programs and support groups immediately, rather than years later. For more information, visit the Baton Rouge Crisis Intervention Center's website, www.brcic.org/.

Linda Flatt lost her twenty-five-year-old son, Paul, to suicide on June 29, 1993. She is now an advocate for the prevention of suicide and is working to improve suicide prevention efforts in her community. In the fall of 1997, Linda became a Nevada community organizer for Suicide Prevention Action Network, a grassroots organization dedicated to the development of a proven, effective national strategy for suicide prevention. She helped establish the Nevada chapter of the American Foundation for Suicide Prevention in 1999. With Nevada having one of the highest suicide rates in the United States, Linda has worked as an advocate there to help pass important legislation designed to increase public awareness and to develop programs for suicide prevention.

In a recent email we received from Linda, she said, "I received an email from a young woman in Las Vegas who lost her boyfriend to suicide on Easter Sunday. Before I could answer her message, I got an email from Los Angeles, from a friend of the young woman who had lost her boyfriend. I thank God that he has provided me with the capability to communicate electronically and that he directed both of these women to me. I was able to respond to both emails with an understanding that comes only from my experience with Paul's suicide. I was able to minister to the survivor, encouraging her to come to my support group. I was able to give the woman in Los Angeles some suggestions about how to support her friend. This is what I call a 'God thing.'" For more information about Linda's ministry, visit www.survivingsuicide.com.

Louise Wirick's twenty-seven-year-old son, Rob, shot himself on November 16, 1998. Louise started her website in 1999 and has links to many other support, awareness, and prevention sites. Through her website, survivors can receive online help, which is available in thirteen countries in addition to the United States. She has established an office in the Dallas area, where survivors can receive help in person. One of her goals is to offer services to families immediately after a suicide. Another is to offer free peer counseling. She also facilitates weekly support group meetings for adults and children and has plans to develop a program in which her team can hold support group meetings in high schools after a suicide. Her goal is to open offices nationwide that are modeled on the Dallas office. For more information, visit www.road2healing.com.

My (Sue's) daughter, Shannon, overdosed with prescription drugs in 1991. Thankfully, with God's help, I have survived—more than survived. Both needing and wanting to make some necessary changes in my life, in 1993 I returned to graduate school and in 1995 earned a master's degree in Marriage and Family Therapy. My goal in getting this degree was to write and speak in the areas of grief and loss as well as to have a private practice. In 1997, I became involved with Survivors of Suicide in San Diego. With that organization I have facilitated support groups, participated on the speaker's bureau, and have been chairperson of the public awareness campaign. I've also led grief support groups at various times through other venues.

I've had many opportunities to speak to young people at the junior high, high school, and college levels about my experience with suicide and find speaking to young people on this topic very rewarding.

One of the greatest joys to come from the devastation caused by my daughter's death has been the realization that what I have gone through has been helpful to others. This includes not only other survivors but also those who want to know more about suicide prevention and how to help suicide survivors. With my coauthor, Dave Biebel, I've helped establish a website, www.hope central.us, which is part of Dave's vision for Hope Central Ministries. The ultimate goal of this effort to mend broken hearts is to establish Hope House, a guesthouse where hurting people can come to find healing and hope.

FINDING YOUR WAY

Ask yourself the following questions, and write your answers in your journal.

1. What would moving beyond survival look like for me?

2. What would this require of me?

3. Am I willing to do what is required? If so, how would I begin? When would I start?

Create a personal timeline of your life, based on the example on pages 144-45, to chart your experience thus far and to project where you'd like to be heading.

YOUR PERSONAL TIMELINE AS A SURVIVOR OF SUICIDE

As a way of visualizing your experience thus far, on a timeline like the one below, register events significant enough to impact you either positively or negatively. (You may need a larger piece of paper on which you could create your timeline horizontally and register the events vertically.) Each time you make a mark above or below the line for an event, write your age (or the date) on the timeline. Make the vertical lines longer or shorter depending on the degree to which each event influenced you. This is just a sample "timeline," for illustration only. Each person's story is unique. Every person's story has its ups and downs.

Events with positive impact

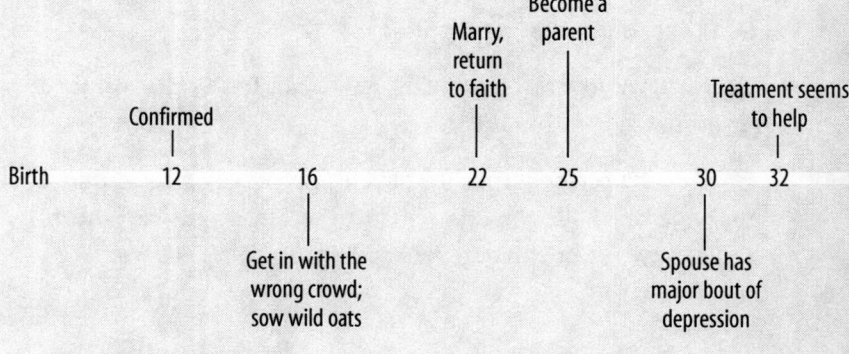

Events with negative impact

Record in your journal what this simple exercise has revealed to you about your journey thus far as a survivor of suicide.

In a sentence, describe where you are headed right now, and why.

If you're headed in a positive direction, list three things you could do soon to continue in this direction:

1.
2.
3.

If you're not headed in as positive a direction as you might wish, list three things you could do soon to go in a more positive direction:

1.
2.
3.

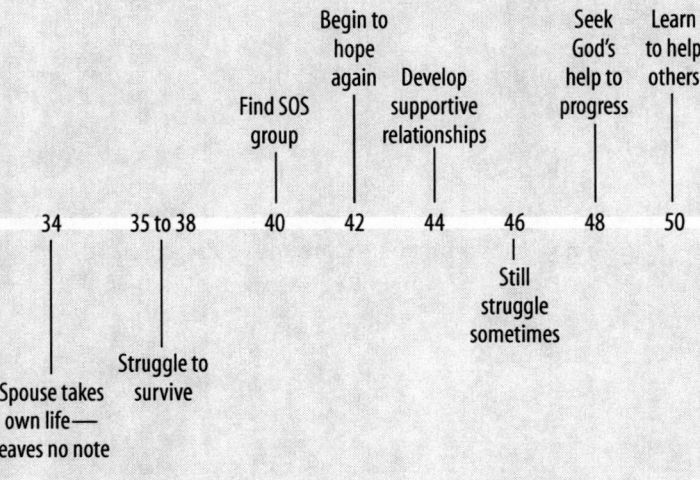

Reflections of a Survivor

A Basic Plan for Survival

Choose to Survive. We must make a conscious decision to be an active participant in our own healing process.

Feel the Feelings. We must give ourselves permission to grieve deeply for a season.

Stay Connected. While on the healing journey we must ask God and safe, supportive people to be our traveling companions—to share our sorrow, ease our fears, defuse our anger, and process our guilt. In relationship we have a much better chance to reclaim our joy.

Practice Acceptance and Forgiveness. We must give ourselves grace and truth and time to eventually accept our loss and forgive others and ourselves.

Slowly Get Back in the Game. All the while, we must gently and gradually ease ourselves back into reality.

Be the New You. We are forever changed, yet essentially the same . . . living, breathing, loving, inherently precious children of God.

Share Your Experience. We can now be seasoned traveling companions for other survivors on the recovery road.

—LINDA L. FLATT, JUNE 1997

CHAPTER 11

Embracing Your New Normal

Before the worldwide GPS (Global Positioning System) was available, ships on the open sea would fix their position at dawn and dusk through the use of a two-scoped navigational instrument called a sextant. One scope was fixed on the horizon; the other on a known star. By using charts and trigonometry, seafarers had their bearings once again.

The experience of traumatic loss leaves us bobbing like a rowboat in the ocean. The typical evangelical message to such mariners is: "Fix your eyes on the things of God, and everything will be okay." Skeptics, by contrast, may suggest that all you need to do is keep your eyes on the horizons—human realities—in your effort to navigate through the ocean of suffering. Though either approach may help to some degree, the only approach that really affords a fix on your position is to keep one scope fixed on God and the other fixed on temporal reality. This is the only way you can know where you are, where you've been, and which way you should be headed to reach a particular destination.

If your goal is to survive and move beyond the pain of the past and toward what might be called a "new normal," keep one scope fixed on your day-to-day experience and the other fixed on matters of faith. Finding a new normal is a process, a dynamic rather than static thing. Yet through our involvement with other survivors, we have identified some elements that foster success in this process. Here's a summary of what we have learned, as well as comments from other survivors, to help you find your way.

Take Responsibility for Your Healing

Friends, counselors, and others may help you as you go, but the basic responsibility for moving ahead is your own. As long as you continue to be a victim and simply let life happen to you, your progress will be slow. But once you become proactive in your own recovery—emotional, spiritual, relational, physical—you will progress much faster. At some point you'll have to decide that while you can't change what others have done or said, you can choose what you will do with what life has handed you.

Healing involves making peace with the past and accepting that you did the best you could with the knowledge you had at the time. It means realizing how little control you really had over events, circumstances, and the actions of others and accepting that there may not have been anything you could have done to affect the outcome. Sometimes all the love in the world can't fill the emptiness another person has inside nor change their feelings of confusion and despair. No one is perfect. All of us have limitations, and part of healing is making peace with those limitations.

Your healing process and its result will be as unique as your journey has been thus far. So while no one can define for you what your healing should look like, other survivors, support groups, counselors, and so forth can be like a mirror for you and show you how you're doing compared to how you might wish to be doing.

Accept That You Have Changed

Some survivors invest a great deal of energy in trying to remain the same or trying to return somehow to the person they think they were before. But you have been changed forever. You can't go back, and there's a good possibility that over time you'll conclude that you really wouldn't want to go back.

At the time Shannon died, I (Sue) was in a job I really wasn't suited for any longer and had no desire to do. This was one of the compelling reasons that I returned to graduate school. Although I was not able to leave that job for another three years, I at least knew I was taking a proactive step toward desirable changes.

Other survivors described similar "life-wide" changes as a result of their suicide loss. Ann said, "The experience has changed everything in my life—everything I believe, everything I touch, everything I do. It's like I've started all over again."

Linda said, "I'm stronger and more confident that I can overcome any difficult experience, because I've made it through what I hope is the most difficult experience of my life."

Mike said, "I'm more patient with others and take life one day at a time. I have become a kinder, gentler person. It is hard not to be profoundly changed by an event like suicide. I am much more emotional and more sensitive to others' emotions."

Marie wrote, "I have more compassion and am not as self-righteous. I feel I am a better person than before."

Lenore said she has become "hugely more compassionate, and my listening skills have improved."

Debbie said, "Every part of me has changed. It took me a long time to get used to the new me that I have become since Josh died. At times I wasn't sure I liked the new me, as I wasn't used to changing so drastically. I'm more serious, not so carefree and careless. I don't take people or time for granted. I choose my battles now with people and issues. I save my personal issues for myself and my family. I am more protective of my surviving children and more protective of myself emotionally."

Accept That Your Relationships with Others Have Changed

Just as other areas of your life have changed as a result of your loss, you will find that your relationships have changed as well. You may find that those you could count on before are not here for you now, whereas others have become the "glue" that helps hold you together. You may also find that you have developed new relationships as you came across others who share the common bond of a suicide.

I (Sue) found that I viewed some of the casual friendships I had before Shannon's death differently after my loss. In many cases, I no longer had much in common with these people. I had no time or energy for shallow conversation.

I felt my life was moving in a different direction, and our values and views on life were now different. I also tended to gravitate toward those who would let me be real with them in my grief and pain and stayed away from those who didn't. My sphere of relationships became smaller.

Some relationships change because others can't deal with your loss. Terri said, "Many former friends could not understand my grief and chose to move in another direction without me. Only a few friends stuck by me."

Debbie wrote, "I had a very good friend that I worked with. Her son and my son were friends in school, and we often did weekend family functions together. She was from another country, and I loved her so much. She was always there for me and my family. When Josh died, she could only stay around me for a couple of weeks. She didn't know how to handle all that I was experiencing, and I think she was also afraid of her son taking his own life also. So she left me. I was devastated. I learned quickly who I could trust and who I could not trust. I have never spoken to her since that last time in 1996. Many times I have wondered about her and why she dropped my family and me the way she did."

Ann said, "My biggest loss is my parents. Although I have not physically lost them, my dad's request not to talk about Wayne has taken a toll on my healing and has given me one less place to seek when needing that connection with my son. It's sixteen years of my life and Wayne's life that I have to pretend does not exist. I was extremely angry at first but understood his request. He had a stroke five months prior to Wayne's death, and his concentration was on rehabilitation and his own daily struggle to maintain and improve his life. He was taking Wayne's death so very hard that it was interfering with his ability to cope with the smallest tasks, and my mother was bearing the burden of her grief and being the primary caretaker for my dad. Needless to say, they were in a great deal of pain and were exhausted at the same time.

"I've also lost some friends along this path of grief," Ann added. "One in particular seemed to be anxiously waiting for me to be angry at Wayne. She constantly questioned if I was and then would go into an explanation of how it's normal and okay to be angry with him. This made me uncomfortable and hesitant to have contact with her. Our relationship has slowly dissolved into only occasional phone calls now. Another friend informed me at four months that I just needed to get a hobby and not think about Wayne and that discussions about him made her uncomfortable and sad. I've had other friends just drop off the face of the earth with no contact whatsoever. I definitely don't have the strength to go looking for them to initiate a renewal of our friendship."

Ginger wrote, "We lost many relationships. Some of our friends totally disappeared after a while. I believe we became too much of a burden for them, and almost all of them pulled away completely. I think that after about a year, many of them thought we should be back to normal. We were the odd couple out, no longer fitting into the definition of a traditional family because our only child had died. They didn't want to see the pain in our eyes. We were even told by some that we weren't grieving right.

"My therapist had warned me that my relationships would change and that some would be lost completely," she added. "I was shocked at the time and couldn't comprehend that happening to us. Sadly, she was right. I wish I could go back and mend these relationships, but I'm afraid I might be rejected all over again."

Judy T. said, "Life shifted, and so did relationships. One of the friendships that vanished was a couple that we saw all the time. They were the only people outside of family that I could trust. Their marriage ended, partly due to the wife's alcoholism, which began shortly after Lea died. That was also the end of our friendship.

"Another old friend waited a year and then sent me a note saying that she figured I'd be over it by now and expected that we would pick up the friendship where we left off. Other people just became too much maintenance, and I let them go."

Realize That Your Perspective Has Changed

Some survivors find that things that used to be important—jobs, material possessions, gaining wealth, prominence—have diminished in value compared to family, relationships, healing, helping others, and living in the present by taking one day at a time. Expectations that survivors have had of themselves and others have given way to the hope that God will help them find renewed purpose and meaning in just living life.

Louise said, "I don't sweat the small stuff anymore, so my tolerance of life's daily issues has greatly increased. Little things aren't as important as they used to be, and life's bumps don't jar me in the same way they did. I make time for my loved ones now, instead of trying to work them into my schedule. I have no problem dropping everything to spend time with them now. I used to worry about how much I had to get done."

Kathie said, "I don't take things so seriously anymore. When you've lost a child to suicide, everything else is trivial. Losing a child is the most horrible thing any parent can go through. My husband is the most important person in my life now. I cherish him daily. I do value life more than ever before. It should never be taken for granted."

Brenda said, "I ignore the little things that are wrong, but I cherish the little things that are right."

Mike said, "I try not to sweat the little stuff and put value on friendships and loved ones above all else."

Linda said, "My priorities have changed out of my experience. I value my life and relationships more, and irrelevant things don't get much of my attention."

Terri said, "The small obstacles that formerly would ruin my day are now irrelevant. Flat tires and traffic mean nothing. I value people and relationships differently. I seek to treat others with respect and tell them that I care about them. Life is too short to hold grudges and be unhappy."

Another survivor wrote, "I found that things were not as important to me as I had thought. I also found that death in any form—friends, relatives, pets, even tragedies in the news—has a much greater impact on me now. The values I placed on things of all types have undergone severe changes. I find myself ignoring a great many things that would have irritated me in the past."

Ginger said, "I have become far more understanding and compassionate of the pain and grief of others, having been there. Before the loss of my own son, I didn't fully understand grief.

"Time spent with family and friends is the most important thing in my life now. I realize how fragile life is and how quickly it can be too late. I do for people now instead of just talking about it, wishing I had the time. I make time now.

"Material things are totally irrelevant and replaceable. Life is not. I try to connect with people more, such as saying hello to a lonely neighbor, doing something special for them, and giving my time to different volunteer efforts. I have become far less judgmental of others. Instead, I try to get to know them and their world."

Be Grateful That You Have Learned Valuable Lessons and Have Grown

As difficult as this learning and growth process can be, many survivors are grateful that it has occurred, as the following people can attest.

Louise said, "I learned how faithful God is and how much he loves each of us."

Judy K. said she learned to live each day to the fullest.

Monica realized that life is unpredictable. "Tell the people you love that they mean a lot to you. There may not be a tomorrow."

Kathie learned to be compassionate regardless of the cause of death or the situation and to be a good listener. "How could anyone not grow from such a tragedy?" she asked. "I can laugh once again, really laugh. And, more important, I can make others laugh. Survivors of Suicide helped me to grow the most by letting me be who I am and by letting me share whatever was important to me at the time. They allowed me to share tears of sorrow without telling me to stop. I learned that I didn't have to apologize for my tears. They accepted me, which at the time was very important. I learned that it's okay to grieve. This experience has taught me not to judge others before first judging myself. I have gone through something in my life that few people will ever have to face."

Mike said, "I think the most important thing I've learned and grown from is how insignificant we really are. We put too much importance on ourselves, our ideas, our activities, and I now realize how unimportant these things really are. The death of my son was a humbling experience."

Becky learned "never to take anyone for granted, as you never know when the next time you will see them and be able to spend time with them will be."

Linda said, "I've learned that God is good and faithful; life is fragile. I have choices. I can become strong through adversity and loss, outreach to other survivors helps me heal, and involvement in prevention advocacy helps me transcend my loss."

James and Patricia said, "Keep your eyes on the Lord because you never know what is next."

Lenore learned that the process of healing and grief is a huge growing experience. "Working on my stuff and facing some difficult issues have grown me greatly."

Terri learned "that we may never know people as well as we think we do. I am a new me and I live in the new normal."

Debbie said, "I've learned that this can happen to anyone, to someone you love with every beat of your heart. I have learned that you sometimes need to listen to your own heart and instinct. You have to go on somehow when your child dies. You have to grow and change through this."

Another survivor said, "Life is very easily taken away from you, so you should always let the ones you love know that you love them at every opportunity."

Learn to Live in the Present

Part of moving ahead is learning to live in the moment, day by day. We call this learning to live in the now, which is where time and eternity intersect. In his book *The Screwtape Letters*, C. S. Lewis presents this idea in the context of a conversation between a senior devil, Screwtape, and a junior devil, Wormwood. Screwtape says:

> The humans live in time, but our Enemy [God] destines them to eternity. He therefore, I believe, wants them to attend chiefly to two things, to eternity itself, and to that point of time which they call the Present. *For the Present is that point at which time touches eternity.* Of the present moment, and of it only, humans have an experience analogous to the experience which our Enemy has of reality as a whole; in it alone freedom and actuality are offered them. He would therefore have them continually concerned either with eternity (which means being concerned with Him) or with the Present—either meditating on their eternal union with, or separation from Himself, or else obeying the present voice of conscience, bearing the present cross, receiving the present grace, giving thanks for the present pleasure.
>
> Our business is to get them away from the eternal, and from the Present. . . . We want a whole race perpetually in pursuit of the rainbow's end, never

honest, nor kind, nor happy *now*, but always using as mere fuel wherewith to heap the altar of the future every real gift which is offered them in the Present.[1]

The only moments in which we are totally alive are those in which we live in the present, savoring the moment. This is because God dwells in the eternal present. He told Moses that his name is "I AM THAT I AM" (Ex. 3:14 KJV). In other words, he is the source of what is and of what will be. In any given moment from the beginning of time to now, this has been true. This is what Lewis meant by "the Present is that point at which time touches eternity."

When we've experienced a significant loss, it's only natural to become so preoccupied with what has happened that we have no energy to focus on what *is* happening or to be thankful for it. In long-term grief, a perpetual focus on what was, and even on lamenting what might have been, can prevent us from ever again experiencing the "now" of our lives because the rest of our lives slip by day by day. When this happens, we cannot gain meaning or purpose from the hope that there really is a larger story of which our life is a part. The life of our deceased loved one is also part of this larger story, but in a more finished sense than ours. The larger story is God's story, not ours, even though we might at times wish to suggest a different plot to the Author.

Let's face it. Either there is a God or there isn't. If there is no God, there cannot be a larger story because there is no Storyteller, and life truly is without purpose or meaning, full of despair, and happiness is just an illusion. Life is, in the words of Macbeth, "but a walking shadow; a poor player that struts and frets his hour upon the stage, and then is heard no more: it is a tale told by an idiot, full of sound and fury, signifying nothing."[2]

If, however, there is a divine Storyteller, then there is a story with a beginning and an end. There are a plot and characters, including us. And it's all going somewhere. Therefore, we can find purpose, meaning, and joy as our own stories meld into his larger one.

Of course, it's easy for anyone to embrace these truths when their story ends "happily ever after." But for survivors of suicide, the possibility of "happily ever after" ceased to exist the day their loved one died, because the story ended another way. Or did it?

About fifteen years ago, I (Dave) wrote, "It's not disloyal to laugh again, to enjoy the little things like the garden, wildflowers, birds, or a good meal with good friends who care about you *today*.

"Can you take pleasure in the friends and family you still have, entering into their todays and even their plans for tomorrow? Simple as this suggestion may sound, it remains one of the most difficult hindrances on the road to wholeness. I recall how—more than six years after Jonathan's death—a dream, coupled with the guidance of a gifted counselor in a group setting, helped me realize I needed to forgive the past and embrace the present. In my dream, a large bird crashed and burned. This was the death of my hopes and dreams for Jonathan. Out of the ashes arose a butterfly—his new life.

"As we discussed the dream, I began to see Jonathan's face, and I thought about what he might say to me, things like: 'I love you. I'm sorry that you hurt so much. Be free. Be happy again.'"[3]

If Jesus were here, today, walking with you, he would deliver a similar message.

Jesus is here. He is the Lord of *now*. One of his most remarkable claims was that he was the "I AM" who spoke to Moses. And if Jesus is the great "I AM"—which explains how he can be the same yesterday, today, and forever (Heb. 13:8)—he was not only here on earth two thousand years ago, he was also here at creation, and he will be present at the great renewal as well.

But the most significant thing in terms of your personal emergence from the mountains of pain is that in every present moment of every painful day, Jesus is here and he is Lord. This means that Jesus was here (and he was Lord) when the event occurred that brought your sorrow. He felt it with you then, and he feels it with you now. He will share that pain with you every moment of every day that you continue to carry it, until you wisely decide to cast it all upon him.

When you finally invite Jesus into the now of your pain, emptiness, and loneliness, you'll hear him gently inviting you into the now of his present peace and joy. The peace that Jesus gives transcends all understanding and will guard your heart and mind (see Phil. 4:7).

The joy that Jesus gives allows you to rise above the painful realities of life while, at the *same* time, truly experiencing the pain. The apostle Paul described his own journey of faith: "Dying, and yet we live on; beaten, and yet not killed;

sorrowful, yet always rejoicing; poor, yet making many rich; having nothing, and yet possessing everything" (2 Cor. 6:9–10).

Live in the now. The story of your life hasn't ended yet.

So the question is: How do you want it to end? If you could look ahead, what would you want to see in order to rejoice that you had chosen to work with God to redeem purpose and meaning from what had seemed a totally meaningless, futile, irredeemable tragedy?

Expect That Your Understanding and Experience of Joy Will Change

Before your loss, what you called joy was most likely mere happiness. It was valuable and more or less attached to your loved ones, including the one who died. But now your understanding of joy is much deeper.

Kathie said, "Joy has a different meaning for me now. I can find joy all around me, in the flowers, in hearing a young child laugh, in watching my dog play in the yard. Joy is knowing that someday I will see my son again because of my life in Jesus. There was a happier time in my life, but that is gone forever. I have moved to a new joy, the joy of waking every morning and seeing the sun rising and knowing that Jesus has everything under control."

Becky said, "Joy used to be having a good time and having good friends around. Now joy is spending time with my family—particularly my husband, son, and grandson."

Sue said, "Joy is finding peace, hope, and purpose in any circumstance, no matter how difficult, and coming out on the other side of pain with a new outlook and a new meaning and purpose in life. It is the hope and faith and the abiding 'knowing' that God is in control and that he will indeed make beauty out of ashes. Joy comes with beautiful sunsets, flowers, music, good books, walks on the beach, watching my cats play, helping others, and my relationship with God, friends, and family. Joy can be found in the pain."

Lenore said, "Joy for me is found inside the grief and pain—the joy found in the God who chose me. Joy is found in others who love you and have stayed by you. Joy is found by experiencing the pain, living in it, and using it to minister to others. Joy is inside the will of God."

Terri said, "Joy is certainly different now because the innocence has been stripped away. Still, I find joy in simple things: God's creation, good friendships, music, worship."

Find and Use Your Healing Community

Healing from the suicide of someone you love is not something you have to do alone. In fact, we don't recommend trying to do it alone, for, to paraphrase a wise proverb: "He who doctors himself has a fool for a physician." It is very important to surround yourself with caring people who can provide support during this time. Terri told us that she was independent before her fiancé took his life, but she found that she couldn't move forward without help.

Debbie said that she needed to know that she was not alone. "I had too many emotions running through my body, soul, and heart, and I needed to know that I was not crazy. I needed to know that this pain would eventually lessen and that I would someday find some peace in my heart again. The person who eventually was the most helpful ended up being another mother who, although she had not lost a child, was willing to let me do whatever I had to do to get through the pain."

Choose wisely those friends who will be there for you and let you grieve as you need to grieve, who will listen to you without judgment, and who won't urge you to just get over your grief. The others who can't do this for you may have to be set aside for a while. As some survivors have told us, needing the help of others was easy. Finding the people whose help was helpful was the hard part.

I (Sue) couldn't have survived without the support from friends, both Christian and non-Christian. In some cases, my nonbelieving friends were much more compassionate and caring than the Christians were. After Shannon died, I was alone when my son spent some of the year at his father's. I knew I had to keep in contact with others and appreciated those who kept in contact with me. My friends were a lifeline for me.

As you choose to move on, your circle of friends will likely change. Some relationships just don't survive a suicide. Sometimes new friendships are created out of shared grief, such as those found in support groups or grief groups.

Some survivors have found the support they needed from other survivors online and have said that this was a safe way for them to be vulnerable because it was online, not face-to-face. You will find a list of websites offering online support in the resources section at the back of the book.

Support from others is available. The difficulty is that survivors usually have to look for it themselves. Many have found the support they needed in one or more of the following three places.

Support Groups

Those who have shared their hearts in this book have found that the most beneficial element in their process of healing was a support group. As Mark said, "The relief survivors feel when they connect with other survivors is the most awesome thing to witness. Mountains are moved, and deep soul fractures start to heal."

Generally, the support groups that survivors find the most helpful include those especially set up for survivors of suicide and grief groups that encompass all kinds of loss. We recommend a survivor group because that is where you can connect with others who can understand what you are going through. The atmosphere in these groups is warm, compassionate, and nonthreatening.

Ann said, "It took months for me to get up my courage to go to a meeting. A friend went with me the first time. Since that first meeting, it has been one of the few places where I find a safe, supportive, and comfortable environment to voice my concerns, tears, questions and can freely share about Wayne without having to worry about the listeners' reactions."

Most large communities, and many smaller ones, have support groups for survivors of suicide. Communities that don't have survivor groups will usually have a grief recovery group. Information on support groups in your area will often be provided by a crisis team when they arrive soon after the death has occurred. The phone book, community centers, local newspapers, and churches are some sources for finding information on support groups in your community. There are also online resources, such as the American Foundation for Suicide Prevention's website, www.afsp.org, that can provide you with a list of support groups near you. Other helpful websites are listed in the resources section at the back of the book.

The Church

Many survivors have found the help and support of their church community to be a vital lifeline. In these cases, people gathered around and offered meals, transportation, child care, and other valuable resources needed in a time of crisis. Some survivors have stated that their pastors were especially supportive and helped put the issue of suicide in the correct light.

Unfortunately, the church hasn't always provided the support and help some survivors had hoped for. Judy T. said, "I had to leave my church in Louisiana and be welcomed into a new community where my scars are valued and respected; a community where I can tell my story and feel loved and not judged; a community where I have been given a venue to share the lessons I've learned, in an effort to prevent youth suicide."

Kathie said that her church "walked away from us. Our pastor wrote us a horrible letter saying that the church wasn't there to minister to us, that we needed to minister to them."

If your church has been a place of comfort, love, and support, you are fortunate. It is important to remember that the church is made up of people just like you and that many people have difficulty dealing with a suicide. Just as with friends and family, pastors and church members often don't know what to say or do. They sometimes say and do the wrong things.

As Randy Christian wrote in an article for *Leadership* magazine, "No one is comfortable with the reality of suicide. No one should expect to be comfortable talking about it or even thinking about it. But I've found that grieving can't be completed, and healing can't come, if dishonesty takes over. Honesty, of course, doesn't mean emotional brutality or insensitivity. The facts can be faced gently and lovingly. We don't have to pretend we aren't afraid, awkward, or hurting. In fact, when we show these feelings, we assure the bereaved that it's all right for them to feel and express these emotions."[4] If your church community has ministered to you in this way, your path through pain to peace and joy again is helped immensely.

Therapy and Counseling

After Shannon died, I (Sue) found a Christian therapist who was a large part of my healing process. He was not a survivor and had not had much experience in dealing with suicide survivors. I found him to be compassionate and caring, however, and a much-needed listening ear. I could unload my anger, tears, and all the other emotions I was feeling and know that I wasn't being judged in any way.

Other survivors have reported that they had similar experiences with their counselors. Some survivors went to two or three counselors before they found the right fit.

You may choose to receive counseling from a licensed psychologist, marriage and family counselor, social worker, psychiatrist, pastor, or pastoral counselor. The important thing is finding someone whom you can talk to and can trust. Your counselor should be someone who will give you good, honest counsel regarding the loss you have sustained and who will walk with you through the grief process. It is becoming easier to find therapists or counselors who have dealt with suicide deaths and who have been trained in grief counseling. Counselors who are familiar with your kind of loss will be able to help you more effectively as you deal with and resolve your loss. See appendix 3 for suggestions on how to find a Christian counselor.

Finding your way after the suicide of someone you love can be a long and difficult process. Thank you for allowing us and all of the contributors to this book to journey with you at least this far. As we part, we offer this prayer for your continued progress:

Dear God,

We pray that something we've shared in this book has shown your willingness and ability to transform pain into power, evil into good. It is possible that at this moment, this reader is considering cooperating with you toward these ends, in whatever ways you may provide. Give this reader the courage to choose to embrace hope rather than despair, living instead of dying day by day. Give him or her a vision of a "new normal" that is founded on a deeper and more realistic understanding of faith and life. Show our reader what this means in his or her individual situation and provide the wisdom to know when and how to begin. Connect our reader with a network of like-minded friends—members of the "hope alliance"—to share the sorrow that remains and the joy that lies ahead.

Amen

WWJD?

In the scope of the whole Judeo-Christian tradition, the ultimate helper and healer is Jesus, whose ministry was foretold in Isaiah 61:1, "The Spirit of the Sovereign LORD is on me, because the LORD has . . . sent me to bind up the brokenhearted." Jesus applied this passage to himself when he announced his ministry at the synagogue in his hometown of Nazareth (see Luke 4:16–21). If Jesus is the greatest role model for helpers and healers, then "What would Jesus do?"— WWJD?—is especially pertinent in relation to survivors of suicide.

- He would say, "You need not be afraid," for perfect love casts out fear (1 John 4:18).
- He would communicate, "I am for you," for all God's promises are "yes" in him (Rom. 8:31; 2 Cor. 1:20).
- He would comfort them by being with them, for one of his names is Immanuel, or "God with us" (Matt. 1:23).
- He would share the survivors' pain, for he was a man of sorrows and acquainted with grief (Isa. 53:5).
- He would bear the survivors' pain by taking it upon himself, for by his wounds we are healed (Isa. 53:5).
- He would never leave them or forsake them, for he is a friend who sticks closer than a brother (Prov. 18:24).
- He would carry their wounded hearts, like a shepherd carries a wounded lamb (John 10:11–15).
- He would gently restore them to wholeness, for "A smoldering wick he does not snuff out; a bruised reed he does not break off" (Matt. 12:20).
- He would bind up the hurt, fill the void with love, and nurture survivors toward wholeness by showing them how to use their pain for good, as he did (Isaiah 53).

If you really want to help survivors of suicide, you could do worse than to emulate Jesus, though you could do no better.

Although this book was written for survivors of suicide, this final chapter is for those who are called when a suicide occurs and for those who wish to provide support for the survivors.

How to Help Survivors of Suicide

The World Health Organization estimated in September 2004 that almost one million people take their own lives every year. That's one person every forty seconds. This exceeds the annual death toll from murder and war. The organization estimates that by 2020, 1.5 million people worldwide will die through suicide per year.[1]

Each year in the United States, suicide claims more than 30,000 lives. For each person who completes suicide, twenty-five people attempt it—an average of more than one person per minute. With each new suicide, it is estimated that at least six people are intimately affected.[2] It is likely that suicide attempts have a similar ripple effect.

Suicide is the eleventh leading cause of death in the United States and the third leading cause of death among fifteen- to twenty-four-year-olds. Suicide rates among the elderly are climbing at an alarming rate.

For the survivors, the aftermath of a suicide is a crisis of devastating and life-changing proportions, as many survivors have described throughout this book. The traumatic nature of a suicide overwhelms the natural human capacity to cope and leaves survivors with intense emotional, psychological, and physical reactions that they are unprepared to deal with adequately. Trauma of this kind can put at risk everything a survivor has previously believed to be real and true about themselves, others, and God.

It is crucial that survivors seek and receive help from others in the minutes, hours, weeks, and months after the suicide not only to deal with the practicalities of the crisis but also to begin healing from a loss of this magnitude. Friends and family, while important sources of support for the survivor, cannot be expected to provide the level of support available through professionals—including crisis counselors, pastors, counselors and therapists, physicians, funeral directors, social workers, support group leaders, attorneys, and others.

Suicide survivors will need:

- Genuine concern
- An offer of help
- A listening ear from someone who cares
- Silence when nothing needs to be said
- Assistance with problem solving
- Empathy
- A positive, optimistic, and hopeful attitude
- No false assurances (for example, "It will be better soon," "You'll get over this")
- Understanding of and tolerance for a wide range of reactions, both in the immediate aftermath of the suicide and in the days, weeks, and months following
- Affirmation and validation of their pain
- Compassion, which will ease their sense of shame and guilt
- The freedom to grieve and ultimately to move on in their own way and at their own pace
- Faithful friends who stay for the long haul, even if they don't always know what to do or say

Early Responders

Police, ambulance crews, coroners, medical professionals, crisis counselors, and members of the media are often the first ones to arrive on the scene when a suicide has occurred. If you are an early responder, you should expect the friends and family to be in shock and disbelief. While you may have dealt with suicides previously, the loved ones of the deceased probably have not. As you deal with the situation as your professional capacity mandates, your sensitivity to the emotions of the survivors is an important first step in the process of their grieving and healing.

Suggestions for early responders:

- Be honest about what has occurred, speaking with compassion and kindness.
- Explain what you must do in your professional capacity. For example, a suicide often necessitates a police investigation. If you explain what you are doing and why you are doing it, your explanations can help dispel some of the stigma and guilt the survivors may feel.
- Allow loved ones time to say goodbye if possible and if they wish to do so, *regardless of the manner of the death.*
- Listen and take time to answer questions as forthrightly as possible.
- Limit your questions to those you need answered in your professional capacity. Anything more than this will be perceived as being intrusive.
- Give practical and helpful information about resources for survivors, such as suicide support groups and local suicide organizations in your community.
- Provide similar information and resources to friends and others who have come to support the family.
- Find out who might be able to provide support for the survivors (a friend, relative, or pastor) and offer to call them.

Pastors

As Jesus came to bring God's presence into the midst of chaos, in the aftermath of suicide, you and other Christians will represent Jesus to the survivors, who are fragile and need to know you care and are there to help.

If, however, you are absolutely convinced that all who die by suicide go to hell, please stay away, as broaching this subject in this situation will not help anyone.

Relationships are often lost in the aftermath of a suicide, and for believers, this can be especially true in the church. Many survivors change churches or stop going to church altogether because of real or perceived lack of support or even mistreatment by those in the church community who don't know how to minister to them. The pastor must lead by example and help the church fulfill its role as part of the healing community: to be an accepting, affirming, patient, and peaceful spiritual hospital.

Suggestions for pastors:

- Manifest grace. Be kind and gentle. Ask yourself what Jesus would do in this situation.
- Provide hope and unconditional love, without trying to fix things.
- Pray *with* the survivors, not just *for* them. Let them know that this is our problem; we're in this together.
- Be available, or find others who can be available when needed.
- Delegate responsibilities that can be shared; involve others in the church.
- Allow survivors to express their feelings, including their anger toward God or toward the deceased loved one. Listen, and let them know you are listening.
- Help with practical matters, such as planning the funeral or memorial service. Survivors often need help in making good decisions, for example, that it is not necessary to buy the most expensive casket or other very expensive options the mortician may offer.
- Give survivors time to recover. Encourage them to take time away from church activities and ministry, and to not return until they are ready, without pressure from anyone.
- Lead them toward forgiveness of the deceased, others, and themselves.
- Erase "I know how you feel" from your vocabulary.
- Be careful and wise. Due to the traumatic nature of the loss, it is not uncommon for the grieving to attach themselves emotionally in unhealthy ways to those who provide the very things they need— understanding, empathy, gentleness, someone who listens and cares. When counseling those of the opposite gender, it is wise to do this in a setting where another person, such as a secretary, is nearby and to counsel in the daytime rather than at night. If possible, allow someone of the grieving person's gender to be the primary counselor. Opposite-gender helpers must avoid becoming involved emotionally or otherwise with those they are trying to help, or a tragedy for one family may become a catastrophe for many others.

The Church

The church should function as a spiritual MASH unit for survivors, helping them recover so that they can return to the battle. However, within two years of a suicide, at least 80 percent of survivors will either leave the church they were attending and join another or stop attending church altogether. The two most common reasons for this are (1) disappointment due to unmet expectations and (2) criticism or judgmental attitudes and treatment.

Disappointment works both ways. The survivor has hopes or expectations related to how church friends will provide support and encouragement. Church friends have expectations about how long grief should last and how intense it should be. Usually, such ideas are both unrealistic and unreasonable, as survivors will likely need support for a year or more.

Criticism and other kinds of judgmental treatment are all too common among believers in relation to survivors of suicide. Condemnation arises from at least two sources: (1) beliefs about the deceased or the survivor's complicity in the suicide and (2) an attitude of self-righteousness, which results in the critic's belief that bad things, like suicide in the family, surely cannot happen to good people like them.

Suggestions for church friends who want to help:

- Provide practical help—such as fixing meals, providing transportation, caring for the children, cleaning house, and doing laundry—for as long as is necessary, and keep what you see and hear confidential.
- Don't just say "I love you, and I'll pray for you." Do something to show these things to be true. Visit often, with no other agenda than the best interests of the survivor. Sit silently with the survivor for an hour or two if that is the best way to let him know you are there for him. Send a handmade card or some other reminder or gift regularly to let him know you are thinking of him.
- Refuse to judge the survivor and refuse to endorse any judgmental words or actions on the part of the larger church body.

- Understand that anniversary dates and holidays are very painful for the survivor. Reach out to her during this time, in person if possible.
- Commit yourself to the survivor as a journey mate for as long as she needs you.

Therapists, Counselors, Social Workers, and Other Professional Helpers

Therapists, counselors, social workers, and other professional helpers play a vital role for survivors in the process of grieving, healing, and moving on. Even if you have not had specific training or experience with suicide survivors, you can help them grieve, help them deal with their emotions, and provide them with medical and psychiatric referrals and with referrals to community resources such as support groups for survivors of suicide or grief recovery groups.

Suggestions for professional helpers:

- Communicate to the survivors that you care about them. If you lack experience with this specific type of loss, ask them to help you understand their needs and concerns and let them know you will try to help as much as possible.
- Make sure they are safe and that others around them are safe.
- Inquire about suicidal thoughts (which are common in survivors) and treat these as you would similar thoughts in other clients.
- Encourage survivors not to blame themselves. When appropriate, you might assert, "It wasn't your fault. You did the best you could." Realize, however, that getting past their self-blaming is more a matter of the emotions than of the intellect, so it may be difficult to reason them through this until they feel forgiven.
- Let them know: "These are normal reactions in this situation. It is normal to feel this way. You are not going crazy."
- If they are clinically depressed, coordinate your care with that of a medical professional.
- Give them hope: "Things will never be the same as they once were, but you will get through this. And, in the future, you will feel better."

• Realize that since you may be the only person a survivor talks to, he or she must be confident that you understand what is said. Ask for clarification when you need it.

Summary

We offer the following suggestions for all who wish to help survivors of suicide.

Don't

• Offer pious platitudes or false reassurances, such as:
  "Time heals all wounds."
  "Everything will be fine in a month or two."
  "You have other children."
  "You can get married again."
  "It's best if you just stay busy to keep your mind off it."
  "I know just how you feel."
  "You just have to get over this and get on with your life."
  "It's God's will. So just accept it."
  "God had a purpose in this, so you should be glad in that."
  "You have to be strong."
• Promise help without following through.
• Share with others what you have learned in confidence.
• Stay away because you are afraid or don't know what to do or say.
• Shun the survivor because you think it was their fault.
• State that the deceased is in hell. Only God knows a person's eternal destiny.

Do

• Encourage survivors not to blame themselves.
• Encourage them not to withdraw and isolate themselves.
• Try to reduce the stigma, shame, and guilt associated with suicide.
• Tell them you want to understand how they feel and the issues that are important to them.
• Give them time to recover, refusing to push them through the process.

- Help them to deal with the facts and to avoid getting stuck in the "shoulda, woulda, coulda, oughta, mighta, if only" mindset.
- Be patient, understanding, and compassionate.
- Listen, listen, listen. Let them talk. Let them repeat themselves, without pointing that out to them, then let them say it all again.
- If you knew the deceased, share positive memories. Do not avoid mentioning the person's name. Allow survivors to say whatever they need to say about the deceased.
- If you don't know what to say, don't say anything beyond "I love you," or "I care," or "I'm sorry. I would like to help if I can."
- If you say "Call me if you need me," and the person calls, get there as quickly as possible, since it is often difficult for survivors to ask for the help they desperately need.
- Make a special effort to remember holidays and anniversary dates. Send cards, make phone calls, or invite them to share a meal. If you are invited to participate in a memorial of some type, consider it an honor.
- Help survivors connect with community resources and support groups. Offer to attend a support group with them, both to learn more and to help them get started in what can be an intimidating setting.
- Offer practical help, such as fixing meals and providing transportation and child care. Be lovingly persistent with these offers. It is hard for some people to accept help, and the survivors may refuse your offers at first.
- Weep with those who weep, and someday you may also fulfill the rest of that Bible verse (Rom. 12:15) when you rejoice with them also.

Depression Self-Check

For each question below, circle or underline the response that has described you over the past week.

1. I often become bored.	Yes	No
2. I often feel restless and fidgety.	Yes	No
3. I feel in good spirits.	No	Yes
4. I have more problems with memory than most.	Yes	No
5. I can concentrate easily when reading the newspaper.	No	Yes
6. I prefer to avoid social gatherings.	Yes	No
7. I often feel downhearted or "blue."	Yes	No
8. I feel happy most of the time.	No	Yes
9. I often feel helpless.	Yes	No
10. I often feel worthless and ashamed of myself.	Yes	No
11. I often wish I were dead.	Yes	No

Scoring: Count 1 for each response in the first column. Scores of 4 or higher suggest that further evaluation should be pursued with a professional qualified to diagnose and treat depression.

—Brief Depression Scale, © Harold G. Koenig, MD, and Blackwell Publishing, Ltd.[1]

Starting Over

Weaving New Dreams Together

For many survivors, it seems that life has ended, dreams have died, and meaning has flown as a result of the suicide of their loved one. Common as these feelings may be, it is possible to start over, with whoever is left in the family circle, and weave new dreams. As you dream together and help each other fulfill those dreams, your relationships will be enhanced because you'll be focused on what could be, not on what was or what might have been.

Complete the following exercise as a couple or as a family.

1. Each person should envision where he or she would like to be five years from now in various arenas of life, without regard to current hindrances to these dreams, such as finances, free time, energy, or enthusiasm. Include as many relevant aspects as you wish. For example, one might wish to earn a professional degree. Someone else might want to leave the corporate rat race by establishing a home-based business. Another might want to retire in order to do volunteer work. Feel free to amend and adapt the five categories listed in the form provided below.

2. After completing your lists separately, identify your shared dreams or goals.

3. Brainstorm about the steps necessary to achieve your goals (five-year, three-year, and one-year increments are listed, but use the time division that is most useful to you).

4. For each goal, plot the necessary steps for achieving that goal on a timeline based on the time division you've chosen (you may need a wide sheet or roll of paper for this).

5. As specifically as possible, identify how you will try to achieve each step.
6. Decide together what your first step(s) will be and when you will begin.

	My Goals	Our Goals

Long-term (Five years)

Physical _____

Intellectual _____

Psychological _____

Relational _____

Spiritual _____

Other _____

Medium-term (Three years)

Physical _____

Intellectual _____

Psychological _____

Relational _____

Spiritual _____

Other _____

Short-term (One year)

Physical _____

Intellectual _____

Psychological _____

Relational _____

Spiritual _____

Other _____

Timeline	One Year	Three Years	Five Years

Your plan (plot
the necessary steps) _____

_____

_____

_____

_____

Your first step(s) _____

_____

_____

_____

When you'll begin _____

_____

_____

_____

Choosing a Christian Therapist

Suggestions and Guidelines

If your physician is a believer, he or she may be able to provide a list of trusted therapists. Names of effective Christian counselors may also come from other survivors who have had good experiences with Christian counseling.

The following questions will help you limit your list of possible counselors:

1. What type of treatment are you seeking: medical, psychological, sociological, spiritual, or are you seeking a combination of these approaches? If so, which?
2. Should the counselor be nondirective, directive, or interactive in his approach?
3. Besides experience with suicide survivors, what other type of training, experience, and certification or licensing would you prefer your counselor to have?
   - [ ] General Christian counselor: (licensed/certified) combining secular and spiritual treatment methods; (unlicensed/uncertified) may include clergy or church staff counselor
   - [ ] Pastoral counselor (certified or licensed)
   - [ ] Marriage and family counselor (certified or licensed)
   - [ ] Christian psychiatrist who does counseling
4. If depression is a factor, will the counselor be expected to prescribe and monitor medications if needed? If so, she ordinarily must be a physician or a licensed or certified mental-health professional working under the supervision of a physician (MD or DO, including psychiatrists).

5. How will the counseling expenses be paid? If through medical insurance, the list of approved providers may considerably limit your options. By comparing this list with your list of counselors and/or physicians you are considering, you may find one or more matches.
6. Does the gender of the counselor make a difference to you?

The remaining questions are best answered in conversations with potential counselors, many of whom will meet with you for a free consultation or do a preliminary interview by phone.

1. Are your personalities compatible?
2. Does the counselor seem compassionate, understanding, and willing to listen, or does he seem condescending, arrogant, judgmental, or overconfident?
3. Is the counselor a "team player," or does she give the impression that her help can take care of all problems related to your case?
4. What is the counselor's primary counseling model and method?
5. If you are struggling with depression, what are the counselor's views regarding the value of antidepressants or other medical interventions?
6. Does the counselor employ a whole-person (bio-psycho-socio-spiritual) approach?
7. What are the counselor's fees? How and when will he expect to be paid?
8. How many sessions does the counselor believe you will need, and how long does each session last?
9. What are the counselor's usual office hours?
10. Will anyone else be present in the office (for example, a receptionist)?
11. What kind of records will be kept (sessions taped, handwritten notes, etc.)?
12. Who will have access to the records (secretary, insurance company, others)?
13. What arrangements does the counselor have for after-hours emergency needs?

Notes

Chapter 1: Why? Why? Why?

1. David B. Biebel, *If God Is So Good, Why Do I Hurt So Bad?* (Grand Rapids: Revell, 1995), 146. Available from the author at dbbv1@aol.com or www.hopecentral.us.

2. Linda Flatt, *Reflections of a Survivor*, "Unanswered Questions," May 1996. From her website, www.survivingsuicide.com. Used by permission.

Chapter 2: Wandering and Wondering

1. Ann Gay lost her sixteen-year-old son, Wayne, to suicide on November 10, 2003.

Chapter 3: Guilt, the Blight of Broken Hearts

1. Ginger Bethke lost her twenty-two-year-old son, Todd, to suicide on July 27, 1994.

2. Adapted from David B. Biebel, *How to Help a Heartbroken Friend: What to Do and What to Say When a Friend Is Going Through Tough Times*, rev. ed. (Pasadena: Hope Publishing House, 2004). Available online at www.hope-pub.com or www.hopecentral.us. Used by permission.

3. Albert Y. Hsu, *Grieving a Suicide: A Loved One's Search for Comfort, Answers and Hope* (Downers Grove, IL: InterVarsity Press, 2002), 91.

4. In Philippians 4:6–9, the apostle Paul gives an antidote for such negative thinking: "Do not be anxious about anything, but in everything, by prayer and petition, with thanksgiving, present your requests to God. And the peace of God, which transcends all understanding, will guard your hearts and your minds in Christ Jesus. Finally, brothers, whatever is true, whatever is noble, whatever is right, whatever is pure, whatever is lovely, whatever is admirable—if anything is excellent or praiseworthy—think about [and practice] such things. . . . And the God of peace will be with you." We don't mean to imply that practicing this advice is easy when you're in deep distress.

But we do know that the peace of God, which comes from leaving things in his hands through prayer, is able to guard both your heart and mind in Christ Jesus. Further, we are confident that practicing the positive and wholesome things that Paul describes does lead back to joy and a sense of the peace of God.

Chapter 4: The Wall

1. Louise Wirick lost her twenty-seven-year-old son, Rob, to suicide on November 16, 1998. "I Cannot Make It on My Own" is copyright © 1999 by Louise Wirick.

2. Bob Deits, *Life after Loss* (Tucson: Fisher, 1988), 123–24.

3. Ibid., 125.

4. See www.health-wise.us for more information about natural nutritional supplements, or write to David Biebel at dbbv1@aol.com.

Chapter 5: Depression, the Scourge of Broken Hearts

1. Robert Walters Sr. lost his twenty-nine-year-old son, Robbie, to suicide on December 14, 2002. See Robert's website, www.fosv.com.

2. For a comprehensive discussion of antidepressants — what they are, how they work, their side effects and related matters — see David B. Biebel and Harold G. Koenig, *New Light on Depression* (Grand Rapids: Zondervan, 2004), chapter 9.

3. Dante, *The Divine Comedy: Inferno,* Canto 34.

4. J. H. McHenry, *Prayer Walk: Becoming a Woman of Prayer, Strength, and Discipline* (Colorado Springs: Waterbrook, 2001), 191.

5. For more information on the nutritional supplement in question, see www.health -wise.us, or write David Biebel at dbbv1@aol.com.

6. Richard A. Swenson, *Margin* (Colorado Springs: NavPress, 1992) and *The Overload Syndrome* (Colorado Springs: NavPress, 1998).

Chapter 6: Preserving Relationships in the Aftermath of Suicide

1. Copyright © 2004 by David B. Biebel.

2. David B. Biebel, *How to Help a Heartbroken Friend: What to Do and What to Say When a Friend Is Going Through Tough Times,* rev. ed. (Pasadena: Hope Publishing House, 2004). Available online at www.hope-pub.com or www.hopecentral.us.

3. For more on how men typically respond to grief, see Terrence Real, *I Don't Want to Talk about It: Overcoming the Secret Legacy of Male Depression* (New York: Simon and Schuster, 1997).

4. Italics added for emphasis. Sexual problems are common in grieving couples. Typically, women experience ambivalence like Marlene describes; men need comfort and the emotional and physical release associated with sexual expression. If this difference is not aired and resolved (the help of a good counselor is often necessary), partners may be tempted to fulfill these needs via illicit means.

Chapter 7: Suicide Survival in Special Situations

1. Lucy wrote this poem in 1996, thirty-five years after her mother's death.

2. Problems with sexual expression are common in a marriage following the suicide of a loved one. Sharing about these difficulties with a confidant of the opposite sex would only invite improper "support."

3. Your own experiences and preferences may differ from this generalization. The primary thing to keep in mind is that your needs are not the same as your spouse's and that sexual difficulties are common in periods of grief, in part because grieving consumes one's energy and preoccupies one's mind. If the problem persists, discuss it together in the presence of a counselor.

4. Judy Raphael Kletter, *Trying to Remember, Forced to Forget (My Father's Suicide)* (Philadelphia: Xlibris, 2001).

5. This list is not a scientific, diagnostic tool. Any of these changes can be symptoms of depression in a child. When a constellation of these symptoms exists, however, and many of them are new to the child in question, professional help is recommended.

6. Some of the ideas and material related to childhood loss in this chapter are based on the work of Pleasant Gill White, PhD, director of the Sibling Connection, and are used with her permission. For a more comprehensive discussion of these topics, see www.info@counselingstlouis.net.

Chapter 8: After the Suicide of Your Brother or Sister

1. Instead of starting with poetry in this chapter, we include this letter from Monica to her younger brother, DJ, whom she lost to suicide on November 9, 2002. The chapter ends with a similar letter from Sue's son, Steve, to his sister, Shannon, whose suicide occurred in 1991. Many sibling survivors have found that writing such letters helps them express certain things that were left unsaid when their sibling left without saying goodbye.

2. At this writing, Marlene reports that her daughter is doing better, through counseling and involvement with Alcoholics Anonymous.

Chapter 9: Questions That Remain

1. Copyright © 2004 by Sue Foster.

2. John 3:16: "For God so loved the world, that he gave his only begotten son, that whosoever believeth in him should not perish, but have everlasting life" (KJV).

3. See Psalm 51, written by King David following his sin with Bathsheba; especially verse 6: "Surely you desire truth in the inner parts; you teach me wisdom in the inmost place."

4. The song was by Bruce Cockburn: "Closer to the Light," from his *Dart to the Heart* album.

5. "For there is one God and one mediator between God and men, the man Christ Jesus" (1 Tim. 2:5).

6. See 1 John 2:1; Hebrews 7:25.

7. This doctrine is based on John 20:22–23: "And with that he breathed on them and said, 'Receive the Holy Spirit. If you forgive anyone his sins, they are forgiven; if you do not forgive them, they are not forgiven.'" The Reformation was, in part, a reaction to certain practices related to absolution (for example, the selling of indulgences). The Reformers' interpretation of Jesus' words in the passage above is that this would be the effect of their preaching the gospel, which some would accept and be absolved through their faith in his sacrifice for their sins and which others would reject.

8. *The Catholic Encyclopedia* states: "That suicide is unlawful is the teaching of Holy Scripture and of the Church, which condemns the act as a most atrocious crime and, in hatred of the sin and to arouse the horror of its children, denies the suicide Christian burial. Moreover, suicide is directly opposed to the most powerful and invincible tendency of every creature and especially of man, the preservation of life. Finally, for a sane man deliberately to take his own life, he must, as a general rule, first have annihilated in himself all that he possessed of spiritual life, since suicide is in absolute contradiction to everything that the Christian religion teaches us as to the end and object of life and, except in cases of insanity, is usually the natural termination of a life of disorder, weakness, and cowardice." See "Suicide," *The Catholic Encyclopedia*, vol. 1, online ed. (2003), www.newadvent.org/cathen/14326b.htm.

9. Eusebius, *Ecclesiastical History,* book 8, chapter 12.

10. Thomas Acquinas, *Summa Theologica* 2–2, q. 64, 5.

11. Martin Luther, quoted in James T. Clemons, *What Does the Bible Say about Suicide?* (Minneapolis: Augsburg Press, 1990), 121.

12. "For it is by grace you have been saved, through faith—and this not from yourselves, it is the gift of God—not by works, so that no one can boast" (Eph. 2:8–9).

13. "Jesus answered, 'I am the way and the truth and the life. No one comes to the Father except through me'" (John 14:6).

14. For more encouragement on this topic, listen to *Chaos of the Heart*, a CD with music, prose, and poetry for survivors of suicide, produced by the ministry of Music for the Soul, www.musicforthesoul.org.

15. David B. Biebel, *If God Is So Good, Why Do I Hurt So Bad?* (Grand Rapids: Revell, 1995), 12. Available from the author at dbbv1@aol.com or www.hopecentral.us.

16. The original version of these reflections by Linda Flatt appear on her website, www.survivingsuicide.com. Used by permission.

Chapter 10: Survival—and Beyond

1. From "Restoring Hope," by Louise Wirick, reprinted with permission from the website of Survivors Road2Healing, www.Road2Healing.com.

Chapter 11: Embracing Your New Normal

1. C. S. Lewis, *The Screwtape Letters* (New York: Macmillan, 1956; New York: HarperCollins, 2001), 76–78, emphasis added. Citations are to the HarperCollins edition.

2. William Shakespeare, *Macbeth,* act 5, scene 5.

3. David B. Biebel, *If God Is So Good, Why Do I Hurt So Bad?* (Grand Rapids: Revell, 1995), 164–65. Available from the author at dbbv1@aol.com or www.hopecentral.us.

4. Randy Christian, "After a Suicide, What Is the Best Way to Serve Those Left Behind?" *Leadership,* Fall 1997, 84–89.

Supplemental Chapter: How to Help Survivors of Suicide

1. World Health Organization, "Suicide Huge but Preventable Problem, says WHO," September 8, 2004, www.who.int/mediacentre/news/releases/2004/pr61/en/.

2. American Association of Suicidology, *USA Suicide: 2001 Official Final Data*, prepared for AAS by Dr. John L. McIntosh, acting associate dean and professor of psychology, Indiana University—South Bend. For more information, see the AAS website: www.suicidology.org.

Appendix 1: Depression Self-Check

1. Harold G. Koenig, James Blumenthal, K. Moore. "New Version of Brief Depression Scale," *Journal of the American Geriatrics Society* 43 (1995): 1447. Reprinted with permission.

Resources and Recommended Reading

Websites

For Suicide Survivors

www.1000deaths.com

SOLOS: Survivors of Loved One's Suicides; provides online support, message board

www.compassionatefriends.org

A nationwide, self-help support organization for families who have experienced the death of a child by suicide

www.fosv.com

Poetry and other information for survivors of suicide

www.fresnosos.org

Help and support for survivors of suicide

www.friendsforsurvival.org

A California-based support group network for survivors of suicide

www.heartbeatsurvivorsaftersuicide.org

A Colorado-based support network for survivors of suicide

www.hopecentral.us

Offers help, hope, and an opportunity for dialogue with fellow survivors of suicide, bereaved parents, people with depression, and those who love them

www.road2healing.org

Online support, help, and information for survivors of suicide

www.suicidesurvivors.org

Help and information for survivors of suicide

www.survivingsuicide.com
A Nevada-based support network for survivors of suicide

www.survivorsofsuicide.com
Help and support for survivors of suicide

Suicide Support, Prevention, and Intervention
www.hopeline.com
The National Hopeline Network

www.mentalhealth.org/suicideprevention
National Strategy for Suicide Prevention

www.oassis.org
Organization for Attempters and Survivors of Suicide in Interfaith Services

www.samaritans.org
Provides support and help for those who are suicidal

www.save.org
Suicide Awareness Voices of Education

www.sprc.org
Suicide Prevention Resource Center

www.suicideandmentalhealthassociationinternational.org
Provides information on mental-health issues relating to suicide

Music for Suicide Survivors
www.musicforthesoul.org
Chaos of the Heart—a CD produced by the Music for the Soul ministry for survivors
of suicide; provides music, prose, and poetry designed to bring comfort to survivors

Other Helpful Websites
www.apa.org
The American Psychological Association

www.nimh.nih.gov
The National Institute of Mental Health

www.psych.org
The American Psychiatric Association

www.info@counselingstlouis.net
Pleasant Gill White, PhD, provides helpful information on sibling loss; not related to
suicide exclusively

Organizations for Survivor Support and Suicide Prevention and Intervention

United States

American Association of Suicidology
4201 Connecticut Avenue NW, Suite 408
Washington, DC 20008
202-237-2280; fax 202-237-2282
www.suicidology.org

> Dedicated to the understanding and prevention of suicide; website includes a national directory of support groups for survivors, listed by state

American Foundation for Suicide Prevention
120 Wall Street, 22nd Floor
New York, NY 10005
212-363-3500 or 888-333-AFSP; fax 212-363-6237
www.afsp.org
email: inquiry@afsp.org

> Provides helpful information on suicide prevention, intervention, and awareness and support for survivors

Hope Central Ministries
P.O. Box 571
Conifer, CO 80433
www.hopecentral.us

> Seeks to bind up the brokenhearted in the name and Spirit of Christ, as described in Isaiah 61:1–3 (NIV), with a special focus on the needs of survivors of suicide, bereaved parents, persons with depression, and all who love them

Suicide Prevention Action Network (SPAN)
1025 Vermont Avenue NW, Suite 1200
Washington, DC 20005
202-449-3600; fax 202-449-3601
www.spanusa.org

> Dedicated to the creation of an effective national suicide prevention strategy

Yellow Ribbon Suicide Prevention Program
P.O. Box 644
Westminster, CO 80036
303-429-3530; fax 303-426-4496
www.yellowribbon.org
email: ask4help@yellowribbon.org

The Light for Life Foundation International; focuses on preventing teen suicide

International

Befrienders International
www.befrienders.org
email: jo@befrienders.org

A global suicide-prevention network based in London, England

The Samaritans
www.samaritans.org.uk
email: jo@samaritans.org

English organization providing support and help to any person who is suicidal

Suggested Reading

Biebel, David B. *If God Is So Good, Why Do I Hurt So Bad?* Grand Rapids: Revell, 1995. Available from the author at dbbv1@aol.com or www.hopecentral.us.

The author seeks to help bind up those who are brokenhearted, especially from unresolved hurts, by leading them to deeply trust God in spite of the dark times.

Biebel, David, DMin, and Harold Koenig, MD. *New Light on Depression.* Grand Rapids: Zondervan, 2003.

A comprehensive Christian guide to depression, including its symptoms, causes, and treatments, for those who are depressed and those who wish to understand and help.

Bolton, Iris. *My Son, My Son.* Atlanta: Bolton Press, 1983.

Written by a mother after the death of her son, this book is a classic for providing help and comfort for survivors of suicide.

Chilstrom, Corrine. *Andrew, You Died Too Soon: A Family Experience of Grieving and Living Again.* Minneapolis: Augsburg Fortress, 1993.

Corrine Chilstrom discusses her son's death by suicide and the deeply spiritual events that occurred for her and her family.

Cox, David, and Candy Arrington. *Aftershock: Help, Hope and Healing in the Wake of Suicide.* Nashville: Broadman and Holman, 2003.

David Cox lost his father to suicide. *Aftershock* explores the relationship between depression and suicide and offers help to both the suicidal and those grieving a suicide loss.

Deits, Bob. *Life after Loss: A Practical Guide to Renewing Your Life after Major Loss.* 4th ed. Cambridge, MA: Lifelong Books, 2004.

Although not written specifically for suicide survivors, Bob Deits provides practical help for moving through and beyond major losses.

Fine, Carla. *No Time to Say Goodbye: Surviving the Suicide of a Loved One.* New York: Doubleday, 1997.

Carla Fine discusses the death of her physician husband, while providing helpful information to all suicide survivors.

Hewitt, John. *After Suicide.* Philadelphia: Westminster Press, 1980.

John Hewitt offers helpful information to those struggling to cope in the aftermath of a suicide by looking at the emotions involved with the loss and how to deal with them and how to live as a suicide survivor.

Hsu, Albert. *Grieving a Suicide.* Downers Grove, IL: InterVarsity Press, 2002.

After his father's death, Albert Hsu wrestled with the intense emotional and theological questions surrounding suicide. He offers help in reconciling the issues surrounding suicide by pointing suicide survivors to the God who offers comfort and hope.

Kolf, June Cerza. *Standing in the Shadows: Help and Encouragement for Suicide Survivors.* Grand Rapids: Baker, 2002.

A Hospice worker, June Cerza Kolf offers practical help for grieving a suicide.

Stimming, Mary, and Maureen Stimming. *Before Their Time.* Philadelphia: Temple University Press, 1999.

The authors present a collection of first-person accounts written by sons and daughters affected by parental suicide.

Share Your Thoughts

With the Author: Your comments will be forwarded to the author when you send them to *zauthor@zondervan.com*.

With Zondervan: Submit your review of this book by writing to *zreview@zondervan.com*.

Free Online Resources at
www.zondervan.com

Zondervan AuthorTracker: Be notified whenever your favorite authors publish new books, go on tour, or post an update about what's happening in their lives.

Daily Bible Verses and Devotions: Enrich your life with daily Bible verses or devotions that help you start every morning focused on God.

Free Email Publications: Sign up for newsletters on fiction, Christian living, church ministry, parenting, and more.

Zondervan Bible Search: Find and compare Bible passages in a variety of translations at www.zondervanbiblesearch.com.

Other Benefits: Register yourself to receive online benefits like coupons and special offers, or to participate in research.

CPSIA information can be obtained at www.ICGtesting.com
Printed in the USA
LVOW041930150812

294381LV00001B/4/P